Bootstrapper

Bootstrapper

From Broke to Badass
on a Northern Michigan Farm

MARDI JO LINK

ALFRED A. KNOPF   NEW YORK   2013

THIS IS A BORZOI BOOK
PUBLISHED BY ALFRED A. KNOPF

Selected chapters in this work were previously published, in different form,
in the following: *Bear River Review* (2008–2009), *Bellingham Review* (Spring 2009),
Creative Nonfiction (Fall 2012), and *Writing It Real* (February 2009).

Grateful acknowledgment is made to the following for permission to reprint
previously published material:
Alfred A. Knopf: Excerpt from *Mars and Her Children* by Marge Piercy.
Copyright © 1992 by Middlemarsh, Inc. Reprinted by permission of
Alfred A. Knopf, a division of Random House, Inc.
Graywolf Press: Excerpt from "Windchime" from *What Narcissism Means to Me*
by Tony Hoagland. Copyright © 2003 by Tony Hoagland. Reprinted with
the permission of The Permissions Company, Inc., on behalf of Graywolf Press,
Minneapolis, Minnesota, www.graywolfpress.org.
Houghton Mifflin Harcourt Publishing Company: Excerpt from "Another Night in
the Ruins" from *Three Books* by Galway Kinnell. Copyright © 1993 by
Galway Kinnell. Reprinted by permission of Houghton Mifflin Harcourt
Publishing Company. All rights reserved.
Jennifer Michael Hecht: Excerpt from "Chicken Pig" from *Funny* by Jennifer Michael
Hecht. University of Wisconsin Press, 2005. Reprinted by permission of the author.
Linda Parsons Marion: Excerpt from "Home Fire" from *Home Fires: Poems* by Linda
Parsons Marion. Sow's Ear Press, 1997. Reprinted by permission of the author.

Library of Congress Cataloging-in-Publication Data
Link, Mardi.
Bootstrapper / Mardi Jo Link.
p. cm.
ISBN 978-0-307-59691-8
1. Link, Mardi. 2. Link, Mardi—Homes and haunts—Michigan. I. Title.
HV28.L57A3 2013
630.92—dc23   2012042425
[B]

Front-of-jacket photograph: Image Source / Getty Images
Jacket design by Kelly Blair

Manufactured in the United States of America
First Edition

TO THE HARDWORKING MEN OF THE BIG VALLEY,

Owen, Luke, Will, and Pete

Bootstrapper

June 2005

HONEY MOON

The thought gradually permeated Mr. Jeremiah Cobb's slow-moving mind that the bird perched by his side was a bird of very different feather from those to which he was accustomed . . . Rebecca's eyes were like faith—"the substance of things hoped for, the evidence of things not seen."

—KATE DOUGLAS WIGGIN, *Rebecca of Sunnybrook Farm*

A perfectly bonny summer morning on the farm and I'm just this side of plowed. Nobody likes a drunk farmer. Or rather, farmeress. Nobody likes a drunk farmeress. Nobody likes a drunk, soon-to-be divorced, in-debt, swollen-eyed, single-mother farmeress, because she simply can't get any work done this way.

It is almost July, the time of year when work piles up like cordwood. I should be weeding, I should be watering, I should be mucking out stalls, I should be turning the compost pile. Last night's honey moon is a waning moon today; time to sow root crops again. Beets, carrots, radishes, onions. So at the very least, I should be planting.

Instead, I grab another beer.

My physical safety behind the wheel of farm machinery is not in any jeopardy, because I'm too broke to own a tractor. This place, at only six acres, is too small to justify one anyway. A blessing really, because right now I could harrow something. I could harrow something real good.

If I know anything I know this: no two states of being entice the unsuspecting female bystander with more money-for-jam-promise than farming and marriage. And I fell for both of them. Fell for them like Scarlett fell for Rhett and Tara, like Isak Dinesen fell for that big-game hunter and a farm in Africa, like Eve fell for the garden snake.

"The serpent beguiled me," Eve admitted, "and I did eat."

I hear you, sister. I took a big old bite out of that very same apple and look what it got me: debt, heartbreak, and perpetually ragged cuticles. The only thing growing here today is my livestock-sized thirst.

Through binoculars I watch my new neighbor, Mr. Wonderful, take out his trash. He lugs, jerks, drags, and kicks the floppy bags down his dirt driveway. His slipper tears a hole in one of them and a buffet of stink dribbles out.

My view of his activity is unobstructed for two reasons. One, because my farmhouse has a wraparound front porch, the kind that invites a long pull on a mid-morning beer, and two, because Mr. Wonderful's driveway is dead ahead.

A week ago this man lived with me; now he lives right across the road from me. In this rural spot on a hill several miles outside of town where drivers are all going somewhere, or coming from somewhere, he's one of my only neighbors. He's also the father of our three sons and my husband of more than nineteen years. We won't make it to twenty. Which is why he's now in binocular range.

"Wonderful" is not the name on his mailbox, of course, but it is the name my friends have bestowed upon him. A name my high-school English teacher taught us was a "euphemism": a polite way to express something blunt or offensive. I have a euphemism living directly across the road. Walk to the end of my long driveway, turn right, sashay past a hedge of the now apocalyptically named "Bridal Veil" bushes, face the road, and there you are—staring at his chipped cement doorstep.

Depending upon your viewpoint, it is either good luck or an epic fail that the place was available for rent when I finally found my voice and said the word "divorce."

Easier for the kids, he said.

Won't need a moving van, he said.

Okay, I said.

When you live out in the country and find you have arrived, through great fault of your own, at a footing so precarious you can barely communicate without cusswords, is having your soon-to-be-ex-husband and father of your three sons living across the road from you a good thing? I'm still trying to figure that out. The beer may or may not be helping.

"Do you think it's been easy for *me*?" he'd shouted, his body ridged and jutting forward in a way that seemed to defy gravity. "Waking up every goddamn morning next to Rebecca of Sunnybrook Farm?"

Perpetual good cheer, it turns out, can kill a marriage. And really, who knew?

What, I wondered, *was there not to be cheerful about?*

I've wanted to live on a farm ever since I was a little girl and my upwardly mobile parents moved my brother and me from one apartment, duplex, and bi-level to the next, finally settling down for good in a "ranch"-style house in "Country Estates." But real farms were where you had gardens. Real farms were where you had space. Best of all, real farms, and not subdivisions, were where you had *horses*.

I am a Sagittarius, of course, the zodiac sign that is half horse, half human, and we want what we want and we want it now. It's taken some doing, but I finally have an honest-to-God country estate of my own. Six precious acres, a mammoth garden, a red barn, and inside it, custom stalls for my two blessed horses.

We Sagittarians do indeed want what we want, and we do indeed want it now, but we are willing to work hard to get it. And anywhere you look around here, that is exactly what you see: work.

I watch through my binoculars as Mr. Wonderful walks back to his rented garage and loads up with the last of his trash, the unbaggables. A vacuum cleaner—the upright kind, with a houndstooth-patterned bag. A burned-out barbecue grill teetering on rusted legs. Naugahyde kitchen chairs with symmetrical rips in the edges from years of swiveling up against their matching table. So that's what happened to the dinette set. When he moved out, he must have taken it with him. And here I thought it was still safely stored in our garage. *My* garage.

His curb soon becomes home to all of the things he took when he moved out but that I imagine his (rumored) Internet girlfriend cannot abide. The same friends who bestowed the "Mr. Wonderful" moniker on him are active online and tell me that he already has a "dating profile." I don't even know what that is.

On top of one of the kitchen chairs he stacks a pile of water-logged magazines (*Hustler* or *Organic Gardening?*—he kept both in his workshop) and a brass floor lamp that looks, with my binocular vision, like someone had repurposed it into a giant bong. But that can't be right. Because if that's what it is, there is no way he would be getting rid of it. He's a smoking man, not a drinking man. Even our vices are at odds with each other.

I scan the horizon and get a surprise. This is not necessarily all trash after all. Because a big sign made of lime-green tagboard stapled to a post is pounded into the ground next to his pile. In black marker it reads, "Free!"

Which is a lie. I can tell you for an absolute fact that someone paid handsomely for all that wreckage, and that someone is me.

A self-help book I checked out of the library on how to have a peaceful and Zen-like divorce is spread open on my lap, making a nice flat place to set the binoculars down when they get too heavy. Chapter 1, page 1 gives this advice: Harbor no opinion on Mr. Wonderful. An opinion means being attached, and being attached means suffering, and suffering means, well, more suffering.

In my Miller High Life glaze, this circular spiritual notion feels like real wisdom. So. Right. *On.* Religiously, I am confused: a familiar state of being I am usually okay with, but one that would be nice to have clarified during this crisis point.

But here's some good news: I've barely cracked open this Zen book and it is already starting to make practical sense to me. Maybe I've been a Buddhist all along, trapped inside a Protestant's body. I was adopted by my parents as a baby, so my spiritual DNA could contain anything. Genetically, maybe I'm a Baptist, a Unitarian, a pagan—or yes, even a Buddhist. Although I have a feeling that pregnant teenage Buddhists were in short supply in Michigan in the early 1960s, when I was born and placed.

From my fenced backyard, our two dogs are howling. Which they sometimes do when Mr. Wonderful is outside. They can't see him, but they can smell him, they remember him, and I believe they even still love him. I've read that canines howl in unison for one of two reasons: either the pack has just been reunited after an absence, or the members remain separated and long for the moment when they will all be together again.

"You two would never make it as Zen dogs!" I slur. Loudly.

This outburst certainly won't upset my few other neighbors. Hollering at your dogs from one side of your property to the other, first thing in the morning and well lubricated with alcohol, is nothing to get your back up about here in northern Michigan.

I give myself credit for picking a responsible moment to be irresponsible. For once, I do not have to set a good example for anyone. Our sons are with their grandparents at the Link family cottage, ostensibly so their mother can "get some summer cleaning done," because it's "summer cleaning time."

This is what my parents tell my sons. They are country boys, but not dumb. They know this actually means that I need time alone to "simmer my shit down." I heard the boys say this privately, to each other, when they thought I wasn't listening.

"Mom needs to simmer her shit down," I heard the oldest, Owen, fifteen, say to his younger brothers, Luke, twelve, and Will, eight, as they packed their pajamas and swim trunks and Gameboys and jackknives into their backpacks. As if their frothy mother were just a pot of soup carelessly heated to a rolling boil.

Well then, I wouldn't want to disappoint. The fourth beer goes down real easy and has me thinking about all the things Mr. Wonderful left behind that *I* should be getting rid of.

Time to purge.

I head for our Quonset-hut garage and climb the ladder into the cobwebbed dark of the storage loft. I peer into boxes, lift the corner of tarps, and open drawers. For two supposedly simple people, both supposedly living simple lives, we've sure managed to acquire our fair share of useless crap.

"What is the appropriate behavior for a man or a woman in the midst of this world, where each person is clinging to his piece of debris?" asks my library-book Buddha.

Appropriate? Probably not for me to judge, but I pitch psychedelic concert posters, rusty saw blades, dried-up paintbrushes solid as clubs, a sour-smelling plastic picnic cooler, a woodstove pipe with an abandoned squirrel nest inside, a pair of rusty cross-country ski poles.

According to one Zen master, all phenomena are in motion all of the time. I see his point, because this phenomenon certainly is. I carry Mr. Wonderful's warped and abandoned jazz albums outside and fling them like Frisbees into the grassy valley behind our house.

"Inner *peace*," I grunt with each act of removal. "Inner *peace*."

They sail through the air like baby black holes, and three nearby crows take flight. I am pleased to see that I still have one heck of an arm.

I pitch a box of his old business cards and letterhead, a scrapbook, file folders of college term papers, spiral notebooks of handwritten angst, lyrics from summer-camp songs, and his high-school track T-shirts, rotting away in a cardboard box.

My selection of cathartic refuse is growing quickly, and I'm already thinking of my own front curb when something even better than trash day occurs to me, and a burn pile takes shape in my front yard.

Once everything is sorted, there is the gasoline gently siphoned out of the lawn mower. Then a match. Have you ever seen what a really hot bonfire does to wedding photographs?

I paw through a box of old CDs, find one by the dominatrix of disco, Donna Summer, insert it into the CD player in my minivan, open the doors, pull up a lawn chair, then sit back and enjoy. Bad girls, Donna chides. Talkin' 'bout bad, bad girls. Between songs, I leave the fire smoldering and head to the basement for more fuel.

And that's when I see it.

My wedding dress.

I tear through the dry-cleaner bag, slip the dress off the hanger, and press it to my body, over my tank top and raggedy jeans. It may smell like mildew, and its princess seams may be decades out of style, but it would still fit. One honeymoon, two apartments, two houses, three breast-fed babies, and an impending divorce later, and it would still fit. There's so little for me to be proud of at the moment that I try to savor this.

The feeling passes quickly, though, and all I really want to do is burn this thing I once spent hours sewing by hand. It is not a custom-made gown anymore; it's just faded satin now, with marshmallow sleeves perfect for roasting on a stick.

Conscience takes over—just—before it's too late. Melting five yards of polyester in my bonfire would probably cause an environmental incident, and so the dress will have to be disposed of properly, off the premises. Some other pie-in-the-sky woman on a budget can probably put a handmade, hand-beaded wedding dress that fastens up the back with antique glass buttons to good use.

I carry the dress upstairs and lay it on the backseat of my minivan, careful not to wrinkle it. I toss an empty juice box out of the drink holder, replace it with my beer, and drive to Goodwill, toasting the Wonderful residence as I pass.

There is a Goodwill helper wearing a bright orange jumpsuit unloading the cars, and as soon as I pull into line, he stares right through my minivan's windshield at me and smiles—the sort of smile a shark might give to a seal. I hop out and slide my van's side door open. Shark puts his hands on his hips, and I can feel him watching me bend over.

"Mmm," he says too loud, sampling the seal meat.

I scoop my wedding dress into my outstretched arms as if I were bringing it out into the light for someone to try on. Time for this dress to face its new destiny.

I will not be attached. I will sever all outward signs of attachment. Like this one.

I look into Shark's face and hold out my donation, giving him a cheerful Sunnybrook smile. He's looking me in the eye, ignoring the dress in my arms. On his orange chest is stamped the word "INMATE" in big block letters.

Disco is blasting out of my car door and Shark grins, showing a chipped front tooth, then does a little shimmy to the music.

"You look like you could use this," I tell him.

I place the dress in his hands, get back into my minivan, and drive for the exit like a woman on fire. Which isn't too big a stretch, since I still reek of smoke from the smoldering trash pile.

. . .

Home from my charitable-donation errand, I return to my post on the porch. Not usually a stalker, a pre-noon boozer, or a drunk driver, I can tell you unequivocally that the way to get your money's worth from a six-pack is to drink it on an empty stomach. Before ten.

God and Buddha should both just shake on it and agree to give me a pass on this rare lapse in judgment. Okay, so maybe sitting alone on my front porch and staring across the road at Mr. Wonderful's trash through a pair of beer goggles is not exactly how I pictured single motherhood. I'm only a week into it, though. Give it time. Because life is sure to get a lot more interesting in the coming days.

I don't have a fancy job, there are two mortgages on the farm, one of which was supposed to pay for a stalled remodel. My bank account is practically uninhabited, and I had to borrow money from my parents just to hire a divorce attorney. My sons are confused and angry and sad.

I crack open the last beer, hoist the bottle in Mr. Wonderful's direction, and drink to this: I will not be attached. I will sever all outward and inward signs of attachment. I will detach right now from the houndstooth and the Naugahyde and the bong water. From the calluses on my estranged husband's familiar hands, and the way he sometimes sings along with our favorite Neil Young songs.

I'll detach from the sound of my name in his mouth— "Mardi*Jo*!"—in happier times when he couldn't wait to tell me something good.

I'll detach from how hard I once loved not only him with my

whole being, but my fantasy of forever with him and our sons, all of us working together on our little farm.

I'll detach from the shock that a love like that can end.

I set my jaw, white-knuckle the empty bottle, and heave it.

And just for the record? I'm claiming my sons.

I'm claiming my sons, the farm, the debt, the other debt, the horses, the dogs, and the land. I'm claiming our century-old farmhouse, the garden, the woods, the pasture, the barn, and the Quonset-hut garage.

They're all mine now, and this is how I will raise my boys: on cheerful summer days and well water and BB guns and horseback riding and dirt. Because I'm claiming our whole country life, the one I've been dreaming of and planning out and working for since I was a little girl.

Last night the full moon hung low and close, like a glistening teardrop on the earth's dark eye, threatening to spill. It didn't, though, and neither did I. A month is a bill cycle, a mortgage cycle, and may become a child-support cycle, but a month is also a moon phase and a growing phase. Our financial lives, our emotional lives, and our cosmic lives are irrevocably intertwined.

If I can follow the moon, if I can remember that both waxing and waning are only temporary, a natural cycle continually renewed and nothing to get too attached to, we'll make it. I just have to stay solvent for thirty days at a time. And then another thirty. And another.

I may not know which God to believe in, but I know that I can believe in us. In my sons and in me.

1

July 2005

WOMAN IN THE MOON

Everything is in perpetual motion; even including a certain young lady in the moon, who was seen with a telescope . . . [and] everything has considerably aged. She had a pretty good face, but her cheeks are now sunken, her nose is lengthened, her forehead and chin are now prominent to such an extent that all her charms have vanished and I fear for her days.

—BERNARD LE BOVIER DE FONTENELLE,
The Woman in the Moon

Take my word for it, burning your wedding pictures in a bonfire in your front yard, then handing over your wedding dress to a snaggle-toothed felon, can take your mind off your man troubles. Oh, it surely can.

But the feeling of euphoria you'll get from this, no matter how glorious, will only last a couple days, or until your kids get home, whichever comes first. And then you're going to have to listen to that come-to-Jesus voice in the back of your head. The one that's been trying, ever so gently, to tell you this truth: that no matter how much bravado you've got, you are not the Lone Ranger, not the lone gunman, and not even the lone wolf; you are just one woman. And you are simply a-*lone*.

Sitting at my writing desk, tucked into an unused corner by the front window, I've got a file folder marked "Bills—Due" open on my lap when my parents bring my boys home from the cottage. Out of the corner of my eye, the ash pile lurks, now surrounded by a black circle of once-green lawn. I can think of no better visual to illustrate my finances.

"How come our yard got all burnt?" Will asks.

It is not some gentle voice from within that I should be worried about, after all; it is just my youngest son's.

"Your mom had a little campfire while you guys were gone," I tell him, enveloping his suntanned body in my arms.

Just eight years old, Will is still one bright spark despite his youth. He frowns at my answer, about to call me out on my obvious fib, when Luke busts inside from the door off the porch, breathing hard, binoculars swinging from around his wiry neck.

"Look at these!" he says, thrusting his arms toward Will. Gripped in each fist is an empty beer bottle. "Mom drank a whole buncha beer!"

Owen is the last to come inside, and he tucks a pair of white iPod headphones into the khaki messenger bag slung over his shoulder and then takes in the scene, unable to suppress a smirk. "Bird-watching party?" he asks.

All three boys look at me with a combination of disappointment and shock, awaiting an explanation. In their absence I've been irresponsible with fire, consumed alcohol to excess, neglected to put a valuable item—the binoculars—away when I was finished using them, and, perhaps worst of all, littered.

"Busted," I say, hanging my head, a gesture that actually seems to appease.

My theory on the savvy-beyond-their-years of my sons is this: because they spend their free time building tree forts, sleeping in tents, shooting the BB gun, catching praying mantises and snakes, going to the library, grooming the horses, and planting sweet corn, they are acutely attuned to their world, and no new detail escapes their notice. Maybe this trait will prove useful in the coming months. I hope so.

At least my own tendency to grudge-hold is not a character-istic I've passed to them. They are of the forgive-and-forget tribe and toss off my bad behavior as if it were just another duffel bag of swim trunks and beach towels they slide toward the washing machine.

Then they relax into home and are swarmed by our wiggling dogs. Friday, the Welsh corgi, who barks and hops up and down over Luke's knees; and Super, the Akita, who swings her wide tail in a circle, puts her paws on Owen's shoulders, and sneaks licks in between his waving hands.

My parents come inside, eye this canine commotion, say "Hi" and "Bye," tell me how much fun the boys were at the cottage, how well behaved, ask if I'm okay, accept my answer, and then they are back in their car and heading for their home downstate.

I wrap my arms around all three of my sons again, force them into a group hug, kiss the tops of their heads, and they don't try to fend me off. Not even Owen, who, at fifteen, often acts as if he's too old for this kind of affection.

"I missed you guys!" I choke out, and the tears well before I can blink them away.

They hug me back and I take hold of their faces, their hands, and inspect them from all angles. They've got sand in their hair, their cheeks have new freckles, and they smell like the beach. They are home and they are happy and there's not a single sign that their father and I split up only weeks ago.

What fine boys they are, I think, *in spite of their father and me.*

They are the fight in me, they are the chapped hands that plant the seeds, the caution that closes the pasture gates, the determination that primes the well-water pump. They are my pack. And I am, and will be, forever attached.

This feeling of family security is so right, so strong, that I know absolutely nothing, not even a divorce, can break it. And I'm closing my eyes and feeling the love when Will delivers a gut check.

"Does 'divorce' mean we can't go to the Cherry Festival?"

Leave it to him to just come right on out with it. Because while I'm floating along in my motherhood reverie, thinking about family and resilience and love, Will is thinking more along the lines of a parade, marching bands, an ice-cream social, and wagon rides through local cherry orchards.

"No, honey, of course it doesn't mean that," I say. "Everything is still exactly the same, it's just that your Dad won't be living here anymore."

I really believe that. I really believe that a family of five can subtract one of its members and then, after the briefest of pauses—

say, for a bonfire and a few beers, or a long weekend enjoying the marital harmony of their grandparents—just continue on down their familiar path at home, the four of them skipping through the woods of their lives together, unscathed.

And I'm positive that this will be our fate, as long as I can figure out the financial part of divorce.

In anticipation of filing, I've stashed cash in a friend's safe-deposit box. This is the take from my occasional writing and editing assignments, tips from a part-time waitressing job that just ended, and the prize money I won last month in the Michigan Women's 8-Ball Tournament. Once the divorce papers are filed, it will be illegal not to reveal the existence of this money to Mr. Wonderful, so I might as well use it all up now. And as soon as the boys are off doing their back-home boy things, I return to the bill file.

I thought I was being so clever by putting money aside like this, but it's pretty clear that no one is going to mistake me for a criminal mastermind. Because after I pay the bills for July and part of August, a total of $122 remains. Financial genius I am not.

But I write the checks, stamp and seal the envelopes, drive to the post office, and drop the stack into the big blue mailbox. The garden is mostly planted, there is food in the refrigerator, gas in the car, a good supply of hay and grain in the barn, plenty of dog food too, so I think the four of us, plus the two horses and the two dogs, can live on what's left over for three weeks if we're careful.

That should be plenty of time to figure something out.

This assumes that nothing breaks and needs repair, nothing wears out and needs replacement, no one gets sick or hurt, and nothing unforeseen happens.

Back at my desk, the bill folder is satisfyingly empty. The boys and I will do this by ourselves. We will live off the farm, I will find more work, and they will grow up happy. Despite confronting our dire economics, I actually feel pretty good. Knowing how bad things are is better than not knowing, I suppose, even when that reality turns out to be a little worse than you'd imagined.

Together, we'll plant the last root crops of the season tomorrow, in the morning light of the waning moon when the soil is damp and the air is still cool. Then I'll take the three of them to the Cherry Festival, just like I promised. Just like always.

And that is my goal. To have their childhoods continue as normal. To give them everything by myself that they would have received if their father and I had stayed married. That "everything" is going to mean keeping our farm, and it's going to mean observing family traditions like the Cherry Festival, and it's going to mean holding tight to everything in between, too.

Whatever that "in between" turns out to be.

By eleven the next morning the boys have finished in the garden and I've mucked out the horse stalls, scattered fresh straw, filled the water tank, and checked the pasture fence. After lunch, I cut the schedule of the day's festival activities out of the newspaper and circle the ones that sound fun. To me.

These include a tour of the demonstration orchard via horse-pulled wagon, then a walk through a cherry-processing plant. Live cherry pie judging, then the marching band competition. Maybe I'll even splurge on the pancake breakfast. I show my newspaper circles to the boys.

Their initial reaction is silence, then universal protest.

"Aww, Mom!"

Translation: marching band music is lame, cherry processing

is boring, and cherry glop on pancakes is sickening, Mom, just totally sickening. Why do I try to get them to eat it every year?

"*We* want to pick what we do this year," Owen, a.k.a. Official Spokesteen, says. "Not you."

When I ask what it is that they *do* want to do, the earth shifts on its axis and now there's actually universal agreement: bumper cars, corn dogs, elephant ears, the Zipper, and cotton candy.

Northern Michigan, and specifically the Traverse City area, where we live, is the largest producer of tart cherries in the country. Maybe even in the world. And so to me, the Cherry Festival is an annual celebration of local agriculture. An opportunity to talk to farmers, see their orchards in operation, try innovative cherry-infused food, and learn more about our area's proud farming history. I have always just assumed that this was true for my sons as well.

Some time in the past year, and completely unbeknownst to me, a seismic shift has occurred. This jolt has caused my sons to rotate their allegiance from me and from appreciating local agriculture, to worshipping deep-fried dough and greasy carnival rides.

Debate on this activity begins, and their primary points are these: they're not babies, they're not farmers, and I'm mental if I think I can force them back into the former or turn them into the latter.

Which makes me wonder. After feeding them organic vegetables and teaching them how to grow them; after demonstrating how to stake pole beans and plant tomato seedlings sideways to get a good root system going; after reading them classic literature in the evenings and playing board games with them on rainy days instead of letting them watch TV, are they just turning out like any old boys, raised any old way, by any old mom?

"I've got to tell you boys, I'm a little disappointed," I lecture from the front seat as we drive into town. "Where's your interest in your native region? Where's your support of Michigan's agriculture?"

Because it's just after the Fourth of July, I've put on a CD of patriotic marching band music and turned up the volume. I hope this little speech will be stirring. That hope, and my sound track, are in vain.

"We don't want to be all historic and stuff, Mom," the Spokesteen says. "We're kids. Duh."

"Yeah, duh!" his brothers add.

I'm the one who made a silent promise to keep our lives going as normal. If this is the new normal, then so be it, and I offer a compromise. I'll take them to the carnival and give them each ten dollars for rides and snacks. When that is spent, we'll all go on a wagon ride together through the demonstration orchard. They'll listen politely to the farmer's talk during the tour and will each remember one important fact about cherry growing in northern Michigan. Then, they'll share that fact with the rest of us on our drive home. An educational discussion will naturally ensue.

"C'mon, Mom!" says Owen.

"Final offer. Take it or leave it."

They take it.

We arrive at the carnival, and a sign on the ticket booth reveals a lucky break. Today is Kids' Day: twenty tickets for ten dollars. The rides require three or four tickets each, so if the boys spend all their money on tickets and none on corn dogs they will have enough for five or six rides.

"Tell you what," I say, handing them each a ten-dollar bill. "You guys buy your tickets out of this, and I'll get you a snack later at the farmers' market."

They agree, and after barely an hour, Owen and Will are out of tickets but Luke still has all of his. He's figured out that he isn't going to be able to go on all the rides, and he can't decide which ones he wants to go on the most, so he hasn't gone on any—not one.

"Honey, you have to choose now," I tell him. "Your brothers are all out of tickets."

"Can we just walk around and look one more time?" he asks.

We walk past the Ferris wheel and the haunted pirate ship, past the potato-sack slide, the Zipper and the Twister, and then Luke leads us over to the games. He eyes an old woman smoking a cigarette and holding a BB gun, standing expressionless underneath a rack of stuffed snakes, looking like some kind of Annie Oakley of the undead.

"Five tickets, cowboy," she says in a monotone. "Five tickets and win this here snake for your girl."

Can she not see that Luke is only twelve years old? A slight and young twelve years old? But he hands over five of his tickets. And she tacks up a piece of white paper with a red star printed in the middle to the back of her booth, loads a plastic rifle with BBs, and passes it to him.

"Shoot out all the red," she explains. "That's how ya win."

Luke takes aim just like I've seen him do at home with his bow and arrows and his own BB gun and starts shooting. This cheap rifle is locked on automatic, though, and shoots like a toy AK-47, wasting a lot of the BBs as soon as he pulls the trigger.

Ah, I think. *So that's the trick.*

This is exactly why I didn't want to come here. And I'm just about to intercede, to tell the old woman that this is a rip-off and my son wants his tickets back, when I change my mind. The past couple of days have reminded me that life is full of rip-offs. Luke might as well learn that now as later.

"Better luck next time, cowboy," she says, reaching for the gun.

Before I can stop him, Luke tears off five more tickets, holds them out to her, and jams the remainder into his back pocket. She snatches them from his hand with surprising speed.

"Okay," she drones. "We got a shooter here. Shooter." A few people drift over. She tacks up another paper target with another red star.

And then I watch my middle son spread his slim legs apart a little, steadying himself, and take a few deep breaths. He exhales, holds the rifle up to his cheek, and stands there for what seems like a really long time. Someone in the crowd coughs and the old woman rolls her eyes and sighs.

"Come *on*, Luke," Owen whispers from behind him, irritated. "I mean, *jeeze*."

Luke takes another breath, exhales again, stands as still as if he were frozen to the spot even in this July heat, and pulls the trigger. A thin circular line quickly appears around the outside of the red star. Seconds later, the star drops out of the target like a dead duck, flutters, and lands on the ground. All that remains tacked to the back of the booth is a white rectangle with a jagged hole in the center. Not one speck of red.

Luke figured out the trick all on his own and beat it. You don't start inside the star and try to remove it piece by piece, because there will never be enough ammo for that, no matter how good of a shot you are. No, you conserve your ammunition and make every shot count.

The old woman rips the target down, takes a drag on her cigarette, and looks at the paper herself this time instead of showing it to Luke.

"Winner," she says, exhaling. Then she yells "WINNER!" at the people passing by. The small crowd that has gathered claps politely, and a big man in a trucker hat steps up to the booth, holding out his own strip of tickets.

The old woman climbs up on a step stool and pulls down a bright-green stuffed snake with white triangle teeth and hands it to Luke. Up close, it's pretty big. He doesn't say anything at all, just grins.

"Cool!" Owen says, grabbing the animal's fuzzy head and looking it in the eye.

"Wow, Luke! Wow, Luke!" Will cheers, bouncing around his brother in a circle. "Can I hold it? Huh? I want to hold it!"

"Nope," Luke answers, wrapping the snake around the back of his neck and over his shoulders like a yoke.

I put my arm around his waist and pull him to me while we walk away from the booth, pressing my cheek to the top of his blond head. Luke is a boy filled more with action than talk. He is my introspective son, an old-fashioned boy of aiming and exploring and building campfires and carving wood with tools, in a new-fashioned world.

I have bonds with his brothers too, but this is the one I have with him. Acceptance of our outmoded life skills—moon gazing, gardening, shooting—is something Luke and I have in common. Together, I believe, we could've survived the wagon trip north, the American frontier, even the Dust Bowl.

"That. Was amazing," I tell him.

He looks up at me and grins his happy boy grin.

"I can't wait to tell Dad," he says.

I feel my chest tighten. I bought him his BB gun and his bow and arrows. I showed him how to shoot them, just like my dad showed my brother and me in our backyard when I was about Luke's age. I tore apart a cardboard box, painted a target on it for him, and tacked it up on a couple of hay bales. All me.

"Why don't you call him and tell him about it when we get home?" I force myself to say.

I am the one divorcing their father, they're not. This seems like an easy concept to grasp until it is you that has to do the grasping.

The last of Luke's tickets are sticking out of his back pocket. He still has ten left. In the excitement of winning, we've forgotten all about them.

"What do you want to do with those?" I ask him, pointing.

We are standing in front of the bumper cars. The sound of squeaking rubber and humming electricity and laughter emanates from inside the ride. There is already a line for the next go-round, but it isn't very long.

"I want to go on these with Owen and Will," he says.

The bumper-car ride costs three tickets. Paying for his brothers to go on the ride with him will leave him with just one ticket out of his original twenty. You can't go on anything with one ticket. He already knows this, he says, and doesn't care. He just wants to crash cars with his brothers.

That is just like him, my kindhearted, fine-boned, middle boy, always thinking of everyone else first. The peacemaker who just happens to have really good aim.

I am oblivious to anything else right now except my happy sons, and how fun this day has turned out to be despite my initial misgivings, and so the next few moments unfold like the clicks of a View-Master, the tiny square scenes a mystery until they arrive, one after the other, right in front of my eyes.

Just as Luke is climbing the steps toward the bumper cars, a long white arm reaches out from the crowd. The arm snatches the tickets from Luke's hand, and Luke's face collapses in confusion. The body to whom the white arm belongs is running. He is running toward me, and then he is almost to me. This is an arm that never sees the sun, never works in a garden. There is an ornate cross tattooed on the arm, and letters—a word?—on the knuckles of the big white hand.

The white hand that just ripped Luke's tickets out of his small one and is stealing them away. Tickets I bought with the thirty dollars I can't afford—we can't afford.

The knuckle word is spelled A-V-E-D. *What is A-V-E-D?* I wonder. *Some drug gang?* Click, click, click, goes the View-Master. I see gold necklaces swaying in the V-neck of the thief's basketball jersey.

Then I feel more than see that jersey gripped in my own fist. A man's chin is level with my forehead, and my eyes meet his shoulders. I'm tall, but I have to look up to be face-to-face with this pale, pimpled skinhead with a scar on his neck and a lip ring.

He smells bad. Of liquor—something sweet, like peppermint schnapps—and old sweat.

"Shit, lady!" he shouts, trying to jerk away. He doesn't release the tickets, though, and I don't let go of his jersey. My whole hand hurts. Or maybe it's just my finger.

"Give my son . . . back his tickets," I say. Quiet, because I don't want to upset my sons. I don't want to cause a scene that could ruin this good day.

My sons are twenty feet away, still in line for the ride, but their eyes aren't on the cars, they're on me. They look scared now, not confused anymore.

"What the fuck! It was just a joke!"

The skinhead is trying to jerk away. Really, really trying. And he is strong, but not that strong.

"Give my son . . . back his tickets."

My hand *really* hurts now. Bumper cars are stopped. Strangers are looking at us, then looking away. Nearby, a ride shaped like giant strawberries is still spinning around in its well-ordered circle. Happy music plays.

Then this person, this skinny, stinking person, looks around, and for the first time maybe registers that we are in a crowd. He throws the strip of tickets toward Luke, mutters "Bitch," and when he lets go I see that his thumb is part of that word, that knuckle word. There is an *S* tattooed on it. The letters on his thumb and fingers spell out S-A-V-E-D.

From what? I wonder. Then think, *From us, if you're lucky. From me.*

If I have ever felt this kind of rage before, I don't remember it. We are fine for the rest of this month and most of the next as long as nothing breaks and needs repair, nothing wears out and needs replacement, no one gets sick or hurt and nothing unforeseen happens. This is something unforeseen.

The tickets are on the ground now, about to be stepped on and probably torn and ruined, but they're too far away for me to pick them up. Even if they were close enough, my hands tremble so badly that I couldn't do it anyway. Owen can, though, and he walks over, grabs the tickets off the ground, and hands them back to Luke.

My sons stare at me, openmouthed. One minute their mother

is talking to them about regional agriculture, the next she is a second away from pressing her green thumbs into a thief's offending eyeballs.

I unclench my fists and look down at my hands. The ring finger on my right hand is beginning to swell, and half the nail is torn completely off. The place where it was a few moments ago is white for a second, then the blood rushes to the surface and pools. I didn't feel it tear off and have an odd thought of wondering where it is. I turn my hand over and see that the nail is stuck, whole, into the skin of my palm. I was gripping that basketball jersey so tightly I tore out my own fingernail.

The gate for the bumper-car ride swings open, but my sons are still staring at me. They step aside and let the rest of the people in line go ahead. Luke is holding his tickets with both hands and the snake he won is still wrapped over his shoulders. I put my right hand behind my back so they won't see the blood, nod a couple of times, and try to give him a smile.

Go on, I motion, *go on the ride*.

They are the last ones through the gate but finally take their places in the bumper cars and the operator starts it up. The other riders grin and yelp, but my sons' faces are flat and serious.

Somewhere behind me I hear chuckling, then deep laughter. I assume it's sarcastic, hurtful, and whirl around, but this laughter is sincere. Just two old men in khaki pants and straw boater hats, tourists—"fudgies," we locals call them—leaning against the snack trailer, bent over and holding their stomachs.

"We was gonna help," one gasps, his mouth open in a smile wide enough for me to see the gold wiring on his partial, "but we seen you had it handled."

I had it handled? These men are old. They should know better than to believe everything they see. Because now I understand that I don't have anything handled. Not a blessed thing.

The four of us are just one swipe away from losing everything: the farm, the myth of divorce being survivable, the idea that I can protect my sons from everything. From anything.

Our whole lives feel scored together as temporarily as those carnival tickets, just waiting to be torn apart.

2

August 2005

BLOOD MOON

As many poems as I have written to the moon . . .
  I would like to shoot along to your ears
for nothing, for a laugh, a song,
for nothing at all,
for one look from you,
for your face turned away
and your voice in one clutch
half way between a tree wind moan
and a night-bird sob.

—CARL SANDBURG, "Horse Fiddle"

Now that he is beginning to settle in across the road, Mr. Wonderful wants to have the boys come and visit him for the weekend. They can choose their bedrooms, he says, and help him arrange the furniture.

I close my eyes and press the telephone tight to my ear and know that he is talking, talking, because the whole left side of my head is hot, but I can't make out exactly what he is saying. His words are garbled and I see an imaginary image, like a twisted home movie, in place of his voice.

He's pulling into my driveway in his rusted-out work van, picking our sons up and taking them away. They sit on the floor in the back, without seat belts, because there's no backseat in this van. No windows, either. They choke on turpentine fumes, because he is not a careful man and has spilled gallons of the stuff, more than once, soaking the fast-food wrappers he wads up and tosses over hunched shoulders. And then he drives away with our sons and doesn't come back, not ever.

Divorce, my father wrote on the slip of paper he folded around the check for my attorney, changes people. An odd warning from a man who has been happily married to my mother for almost half a century.

But Mr. Wonderful is not a treacherous person and I'm not usually so prone to conspiracy theories. And yet, I can't help it, I wonder if their father finagled his across-the-road rental as a ruse to steal our sons.

And then the false image fades, my father's note fades, and I am hearing my husband's voice again, his words are perfectly clear, and he's saying he misses our boys something awful. And I know immediately that this is fact, this is truth, and it trumps my doomsday scenario. I hear the father he is to our sons in his voice and my chest aches for him. For us.

This empathy is good for about, oh, maybe fifteen seconds.

Because when I hang up the phone and ask the boys if they'd like to go visit their father in his new place for the whole weekend, they say "Yes," just like that, the little traitors.

"Mom is like all *Neg*atron now," Luke, a fan of the nifty Transformers quick-change toys, hisses in warning to his brothers while I boil their tomato soup and burn their grilled cheese sandwiches.

He's nailed it, too, because I'm pretty sure this is exactly what it would feel like to be possessed by a giant alien robot. For counsel on how to deal with this strange affliction, I turn not to my Buddhist library book but to my SMILE handbook. Mr. Wonderful and I have both attended something called the SMILE Program, an evening workshop mandatory in Michigan for divorcing couples with children. SMILE stands for Start Making It Livable for Everyone.

"Anger, disappointment, hurt, grief and *a desire for revenge* [italics mine] are some normal reactions to separation and divorce," the handbook states.

I want to be this mother that SMILE holds out as the ideal: the one who adapts and copes and puts the needs of her children first. I don't feel like this mother, though, and I sure don't feel normal, either. I feel small and mean and dark and out of control.

The boys leave with their father right after our scorched-earth dinner, on foot, with Will even skipping and looking up at him and smiling. In their absence, I try to meditate, or pray, or accomplish some combination of both, but all I manage to do is brood.

Our farmhouse has been torn apart by the remodeling project, but the builder is gone now, because I don't have the money to pay him to put it back together again. We were going to have a master suite with a new bedroom, a new tiled bathroom, a walk-in closet, and a balcony. Now there's just an unfinished staircase, a bedroom with no trim or furniture, and a bathroom with no plumbing.

The big, open rooms don't keep things inside themselves anymore; and as I sit here in my flowered chair, eyes closed, shoulders that keep insisting on tensing themselves up to my earlobes, the house sounds different.

Our Father, who art in heaven, I think, trying out this prayer as a kind of mantra, *please let my sons stay whole.*

But the dogs pant, the well pump clicks off and then back on, and I even hear the bumblebees outside, pollinating away as if everything were on schedule, and I can't focus. Because nothing is on schedule for me when the boys aren't here, and even sound behaves differently without their constant voices around to fill up the space.

It's been two months since my front-lawn bonfire and the grass has since grown back, green as ever. The idea that the hurt I feel over the end of my marriage can be healed just as quickly is tantalizing. Even if a lot of what I read—like this, for example— only mystifies me:

"Before I had studied Zen, I saw mountains as mountains, and waters as waters. When I arrived at a more intimate knowledge, I saw that mountains are not mountains, and waters are not waters. But now I see mountains once again as mountains, and waters once again as waters."

I think on this and try my made-up mantra again—*Our Father, who art in heaven, please let my sons stay whole*—but it's impossible to appreciate the solitude when all I feel is the loneliness. An emotion that seems to have no theological, geographical, or sociological boundaries. The SMILE handbook addresses it, the Bible addresses it, and so does my growing collection of Zen lit.

According to the Buddhist nun Pema Chödrön, there isn't just one kind of loneliness; there are actually *six* different kinds, and a self-diagnosis reveals that I suffer from all of them. I want too much, feel too much, expect rescue, lack discipline, assign blame, and, most of all, I brood. And it's kind of good to know that an emotion that feels uncontrollable is documented so rationally.

It's still dark outside when I'm reading about all of this; I've gotten up at dawn, because without the boys here, sleep is impossible. I make coffee, get dressed, and take refuge in the barn.

Here is the one place where I do still feel normal. The smell of new hay, and the presence of big, warm bodies expecting me, and the sound of my horses' grassy, even breath is the only thing that calms. I feed Major and Pepper their grain as the sun comes up, and I listen to them chew.

When they're both finished eating I give them a brush-down, comb burrs out of their tails, pick compacted dirt and pebbles out of their hooves, and then turn them out into the pasture.

They trot over into the shade of a giant red pine just the way they do every morning, because nothing has changed for them, and they press their bodies together to each other, nose to tail. I can feel their simple equine contentment, and it might even be catching—that Zen book should probably be titled *Chop Wood, Carry Water, Care for Horses.*

They are like a balm for my bruised heart, my horses are this morning. I've wanted to have my own horses ever since my parents took my brother, Ben, and me on a summer vacation to visit distant relatives out west. Our father's cousins owned an honest-to-God ranch with an honest-to-God name, the Bar F. I was so proud to learn back then that ranching was, at one time anyway, the Link family business. And right then I decided I would have horses when I grew up. It was a girlhood dream I've kept close at hand for more than three decades—one I was finally able to realize two years ago.

I watch Major and Pepper nuzzle each other for a few more minutes as the daylight spreads, then top off their water tank and check the charge on the electric fence. On the way back to the house, I open up the valve on the garden sprinkler, listen to the syncopated bursts of water, then take up my post back on the porch, my lap heavy with library books again.

And the loneliness returns as if it's been sitting here in one of my empty chairs just waiting for me. At least this time when I greet the new day here, my beverage of choice is coffee.

"When you wake up in the morning and out of nowhere comes the heartache of alienation and loneliness, could you use that as a golden opportunity?" the Buddhist nun asks. "Right there in the moment of sadness and longing, could you relax and touch the limitless space of the human heart?"

Well, I can sure try.

I can try not to brood, and I can try to relax instead, even if I am oblivious to the existence of the place inside she calls the "limitless space of the human heart." That's pretty woo-woo for me, but I am about to close my eyes and try to find it anyway when movement in the yard catches my bloodshot eye.

An injured water bird is skulking around the yard, looking lost. He is an obvious interloper; the Grand Traverse Bay is three miles north and the closest inland lake is at least two miles east. The only water on my whole property is a little koi pond near the south end of the porch.

The bird's black form darts over the grass, and his contorted shadow makes me think not of my own shadow self but rather of Edgar Allan Poe's Raven. This bird showed up just in time to spare me another failed attempt at relaxing, meditation, or anything of the like.

And really, if this were a full working farm, there wouldn't be time for such feckless pursuits anyway. In an attempt to move in that direction, I have recently named my place the Big Valley, in homage to the television ranch of my youth. After our family trip out west in the 1970s, I practically worshipped reruns of that show.

Now I imagine that on my best days I am just like Victoria Barkley, the Barbara Stanwyck role—tough, resourceful, impervious to naysayers. Even with modern life trying to press in, my sons could do worse than to turn out like Jarrod, Nick, and Heath when they grow up—hardworking, independent, and fair-minded.

They're not here, though; this new bird character is, and he needs a name. I'll call him Edgar and pretend that the boys are just off on a two-day roundup and that someone up there sent this damaged avian guest my way to keep me company until they come home.

He is crow-sized and looks all black from a distance, but when he ventures closer I see that he has streaks of brown and tan on his breast, yellow legs, and white shoulders that are mostly hidden by the black feathers covering the rest of his wings. I'm sure he's injured, because he doesn't fly, just runs. Advancing toward my koi pond at a forward incline, he leads with the most dominant part of his armature, his saber-like beak.

When he hops on a rock, then wades in, I fetch my Roger Tory Peterson, the classic bird guide I keep handy on the kitchen windowsill.

I flip through the color plates and learn that he is a green heron, a secretive, carnivorous, and solitary relative of the more common great blue heron. The book says that green herons are native to the Midwest, and I know my birds, but I still don't remember ever seeing one like him before, at least not up close. I read on and learn that's because his status is "threatened" due to "human disturbance."

I feel you, Edgar. *The Big Valley* specialized in human disturbance. The boys and their mother got along fine every week, loading the wagons and riding fence and breaking the broncos and having sing-alongs by the campfire. It was other people who messed everything up. And it is not lost on me that there was no Mr. Barkley.

Outside, Edgar is enjoying the pond, and I take this as an unintended compliment. I designed, dug, built, plumbed, and landscaped that pond myself, shoehorning it into a narrow twelve-foot space between a brick walkway and an ivy-covered fence. I filled it with koi and added a waterfall, planning for the sound of moving water and the reflection of light to give off a welcoming mood next to the porch steps and my front door. This rare bird totally gets it. And I'm happy to see my efforts have actually faked out nature.

Edgar stands very still then, one yellow-rimmed eye staring down at the water. A quick lunge and there is a speckled koi struggling on the end of his beak. In two hunched gulps the young fish is gone. I watch from the porch as the other fish speed to the bottom and school together. Crap.

I didn't fake out nature at all—it faked out me. And nature, unfortunately, kills stuff. As a rural person, I should know this. I *do* know this, and usually take the appropriate precautions.

I protect the corn seeds from the crows, the dogs from ticks, and my horses from roundworms and the strangles. I hope I'll be able to protect my sons from the flaws of their mother, but in their absence I'll protect my imported pet-store fish from a threatened native bird. This is the Big Valley and, endangered or not, this trespasser is not going to eat any more of my koi.

I shoo Edgar away from the pond, across the yard, and down into my woods, where foxes, feral cats, and coyotes are known to prowl.

My bird book says that in another month Edgar should be migrating south. With that injured wing and no food source, his chances of making it aren't good. Despite his outward bravado, he's a fragile creature, all alone, and at the mercy of human disturbance. Mine.

Late that night, or maybe early, early morning, a thick sound wakes me up. It has the feel of an impact, like someone falling out of bed or down the stairs. Someone heavy. Too heavy for the black vampire bird of my bad dream, returned in my sleep from the woods, bloody and rotting, to peck down our farmhouse's door.

Half-asleep, I call out, "Boys?"

The house is quiet.

"Boys?" I call again, climbing out of bed, climbing out of sleep, climbing out of that half-remembered dream. And then I'm down my unfinished stairway, hopping over the central landing, up the boys' stairway and almost to the other side of the second floor and their bedrooms, when I remember. They are still across the road at their father's. I am in the house alone, and there's no one here but the dogs and me.

Super, our Akita, has a guard dog's suspicious nature and would bite an intruder without so much as snarling at him first, but Friday, our corgi, is a herding dog, and he would run circles around a trespasser and bark and bark. I haven't heard so much as a whine, though, and check the mudroom. The dogs are both asleep on their rugs, and so I know for drowsy certain that the house is unbreached.

With the remodel only half done, the kitchen ceiling is still stripped to its lathing, there are fistlike holes where light fixtures are supposed to be, and the stairway is just raw wood and open to the kitchen. The house has changed its olden voice, and sound echoes differently now from room to room and floor to floor. Something feels off, but maybe what I heard was just a sheet of drywall stored somewhere, perhaps leaned against the basement wall, falling to the floor.

It's a muggy night, I've left the windows open, and just when I think I either imagined the sound or that even if I didn't it isn't anything to worry about, I hear sirens on the road. They're close, and so I walk outside in my nightgown to see what brought them here.

The details of the next several minutes blur. Do I hear or see the sheriff's car park in front of my house? I'm not sure, it just isn't there, and then in another glance it is. I might run outside, straight to the side of the road, or maybe I just walk, still hopeful this is someone else's nightmare.

My next memory is a well-defined one, though, even if I wish it weren't. Blue and red lights are blinking on the bare skin of my arms as I sit cross-legged in the grass between the pasture and the road. There's a lawman standing up next to his car, door flung open, talking on his car radio.

My nightgown sticks to my thighs and my horse Major's head is in my lap.

He's lying by the side of the road next to me, groaning, and I am kissing his velvet nose, and even though it is a suffocating and humid night in August, I can't stop shivering.

And at first, I don't know anything. Not how to breathe, not how to relax my throat so the scream can get out, not what just happened, or why, or who called the police.

And I actually try to ask. I try to ask who called them, as if this were somehow important, but I feel my whole body shake, and I gag on the metal smell of all that blood as it pumps down my shins, and I can't get the words out.

I press my forehead to my horse's white blaze instead, bury my mouth against bone and hair, and his last-ever gesture to me isn't a nicker or a head shake or a tail swish, it's just to muffle my sobs with his wide neck.

Major is dying, my dream of horses is dying, or I am dying, or maybe all three.

And it is a single line of poetry I remember at this wrong moment that saves me, just, from that death blow: "First I would like to write for you a poem to be shouted in the teeth of a strong wind."

A horse's head is heavy, but I focus on this one harmless line of words instead of thinking about the weight, instead of petting his Roman nose, the one that the horse trader said was a flaw but that I fell instantly in love with after just one test ride around the arena. I focus on that line instead of the intelligent face of his that I attached to in an instant, handing over the birthday money my mother gave me to buy him, more than thirty years after I first asked her for a horse.

And I am watching all this from way high up, as if I were actually on the moon instead of seeing a crescent of it reflected in Major's wide-open eye. As if I were floating and not sitting here next to my horse and holding him while he dies. Because up here, I can just flick that line of poetry straight down to some other woman and some other horse like a lead rope tossed out for a last-second rescue.

But now is not the time for poetry, or the time for rescue, either. Now is the time for this woman to put her girlish dreams aside. For her to realize that the sound that woke her up was real. The copper smell of blood soaking my nightgown is real, and the police are real, and the impact was real, too. As real as the front of a truck connecting with the broad side of horseflesh at, the sheriff says, a reasonably high rate of speed.

And for the first time I notice two people sitting in the front seat of a smashed-up truck, staring straight ahead, and the sheriff puts his hand on my shoulder and says not to worry any, because the people are badly shaken but unhurt.

Another deputy arrives in his cruiser, leaves the lights flashing but shuts the siren off the way they do when speed is no longer necessary. The two men confer. One gets back on the radio and I see his lips move, see him recite my address, and I am tied right here to the present but I want to go back to that trip out west.

I want to go back to the time when the only thing real about a horse was my dream of having one. A horse that existed only in my longing for him, and not the horse who is here, who is beloved, whom I recite poetry to, and who, even though I know I get every word of that poem right, is still dying by the side of the road.

I look across his body, across the road, and see no lights on at the Wonderful residence.

Please, God. Please don't let the boys wake up and see this. Please.

I cup Major's soft ear in my palm and choke out that line: "I would like to write for you a poem to be shouted in the teeth of a strong wind."

His breath leaves him in a sigh, I feel him relax, and I think—no, I know—that all the horse dreams of my girlhood are dead now. My marriage is dead, my dreams are dead, and my real horse is dead, too. And no one comes outside from the Wonderful house, because that is an easy prayer to answer.

Then the deputy fills out some paperwork for me to sign, and soon everyone is gone. The two deputies, the people staring straight ahead, their smashed-up truck, the tow truck, and my horse, too. Gone.

When I went to sleep last night, I had a horse named Major. Then I woke up. And all that's left of him is a destroyed spot in the grass shaped exactly like a horse in mid-gallop. Yesterday morning, I thought I was lonely. Not just lonely, but six different kinds of lonely. I stare at the awful wound in the dirt and know that until this second, I didn't even know what that word meant.

Something else, though, is absolutely clear: this is the limitless space of the human heart.

I walk away from the road, up the front steps, and into my empty farmhouse like a sleepwalker. I'm sticky with horsehair and dried blood, and my dogs smell it on me and must feel afraid, even lionhearted Super, because they crawl toward me on their bellies. I put my hands on their warm heads, stand in my dark kitchen, and hug that dumb and hopeful girl goodbye.

My memory delivers the next couple of lines from that poem then, and I just let them come.

> *The road I am on is a long road and I can go hungry*
> *again like I have gone hungry before.*
> *What else have I done nearly all my life than go hungry*
> *and go on singing?*

. . .

The sun actually comes up the next morning, and the one after that, too. Two days without Major and I can tell that Pepper already knows from lonely. She has pawed and stamped a deep hole in her stall, I went to Tractor Supply and bought a bag of her favorite treats, but she still won't eat. Horses are herd animals, a holdover from days when they were more likely to meet their end by a wolf's fang or a cougar's claw and not the front end of a dual-axle pickup truck. They get anxious and lonely if kept all by themselves, I am in no position to buy another horse, and so I sell Pepper and most of my horse tack to a tourist ranch down the road.

The boys ask me if we can go and visit her, and three times I make arrangements to, but when the time comes I am still too broken and can't bring myself to see her again, and I make up excuses. After a few weeks, my sons don't ask me about her anymore.

And even though she is getting good care, I hear from a friend of a friend that Pepper is not adjusting well to her new home. She is allowed to leave the barn and accompany groups of trail riders, but since she is new to this ranch, and untried, she isn't saddled up and assigned a rider. Instead, she is just patronized, and clipped behind one of the wranglers' horses by her halter.

One day, these trail riders head out as usual, but Pepper is left behind in a pasture. Just an oversight, probably. But she watches this group leave the ranch without her, panics when they round a bend into the woods and out of her sight, and it takes some time and some doing but she is determined and eventually she escapes the fence. She doesn't catch up to the group of riders, though, and the wranglers only notice that she is missing when they return to the barn at the end of the day.

It had been rainy for several days when Pepper found her way out of that pasture, and the wranglers find her just before dark, stuck in a mud hole in the woods up to her chest. She is in so deep, she has to be pulled out with a tractor. Remarkably, she is unharmed, no broken legs, no broken anything. At least nothing visible.

The ranch people say they have no idea why a smart old horse like Pepper would do something so nutty. But I know why. As a matter of fact, I know six kinds of lonely reasons why.

3

September 2005

HARVEST MOON

. . . Home where I sit in the glider, knowing it needs oil,
like my own rusty joints. Where I coax blackberry
to dogwood and winter to harvest, where my table
is clothed in light. Home where I walk out on the thin
page of night, without waving or giving myself away,
and return with my words burning like fire in the grate.

—LINDA PARSONS MARION, "Home Fire"

Out west on real ranches, real ranchers have so much fence to check on, they do it from horseback and call it "riding fence." They look for rusted-through barbed wire, injured cattle, and wolf tracks.

I used to fancy myself "walking fence" every week or so when I'd circle the perimeter of our two-acre pasture in my knee-high rubber boots. I'd look for tall weeds breaking the electrical circuit, anything dangerous to horses' hooves that might be lurking in the ground, and broken or damaged fence wire. But there's no reason for me to make that weekly walk anymore.

After Major was hit, I did find a spot in the fence where the fence posts were bent almost to the ground but the drooping electric wire was still intact, still "hot." There were hoofprints gouged deep in the dirt, and looking down at them I could feel his panic.

I've had a few sightings of a skinny, mange-pocked German shepherd–like dog I've never seen before trotting in the pasture—sniffing the air, hackles up, sometimes digging or pawing at the ground. I watch him from the fenced-in safety of the garden and know I am looking at a killer. He is the reason Major was in the middle of the road in the middle of the night.

One day while the kids are at school I sit down next to my empty barn, lean my back against a warm outside wall in the sun, and face the pasture. Luke's BB gun is across my knees and there's a golf club in my hand. The gun is to take the dog down and the club is to finish him off. Tender heart that I am, I could do it. I think I might actually *like* doing it.

But the dog doesn't show. Not today, and not ever. I leave the golf club handy, just in case.

Since the tourist ranch's truck pulling the horse trailer with Pepper's tail swinging out the back window exited the driveway, I haven't kept up with any of the regular chores. Walking fence, mucking out the stalls, and grooming the horses used to be my favorite ones; now I don't have to do them anymore.

And the other work here feels without purpose. There are weeds in the garden, the grass isn't mowed, and carrots, squash, and the last of the tomatoes need to be harvested. The builder calls on the phone, but I don't answer and he leaves a message asking when I'd like to meet with him to discuss the unfinished remodeling project. I don't call him back.

Instead of working outside, I keep pretty much to the house. Inside the house, I keep pretty much to a flowered chair in front of the picture window. Curled up, legs stiff as an old woman's on a rainy day, I keep pretty much to myself.

There is no one to pray to these days, though I revisit the Buddhism books to see if subsequent readings bring any understanding. Are mountains really mountains or aren't they? Are waters waters, or what? Thich Nhat Hanh says deep sadness comes from being attached to a flawed sense of coming and going. If I am doing either, I can't put a finger on which one it is. I read the Book of Job a couple times through in awe. My faith is tiny. It could not withstand even one of those sadistic tests. I would fail. I feel like I have already failed.

I watch my sons out the window pick the ripe carrots, snap peas, and sweet corn that I've ignored, eating them raw right out there in the garden, dirt and all. In another lifetime, such antics would send me for the camera. Now, I can't get out of my chair.

There are still a few warm days left before fall, and in the late afternoon when they get off the schoolbus, the boys set down their backpacks, take off their shirts and shoes, and run through the sprinkler in their shorts or jeans to cool off.

We live only three miles from Grand Traverse Bay and one of the most beautiful freshwater beaches in the Midwest, but all my kids get is our low-pressure, well-water sprinkler. I don't have the energy or the gas money for the beach. I don't have the internal drive or focus for editing and writing work, either, and assignments are overdue.

Through the screen door I hand the boys sandwiches wrapped

in squares of wax paper and Baggies full of apple slices. I watch them swordfight with sticks and make thumb whistles out of the variegated blades they rip from the landscape grasses around the pond. I can hear them out there, making a weird sound as if they were all out of breath. I have to think about it before I realize what it is. Laughing.

Blue jays are gorging themselves on the sunflower heads in the garden, tent-worm caterpillars make skeletons out of the elm tree, and late-season growth sprouts from the jack pines out by the road. These new pine branches grow in between the old ones and stick straight up, just like a middle finger. It feels like even the trees are flipping me off.

And I learn that a lowland jungle of leaves and vines have taken over the pasture on a Saturday when I hear one of the boys crying.

"Mom!" comes the sobbing holler from outside. It sounds like Will. And it sounds like he just said, "Luke squashed my head!"

I think of Luke's precision with the BB gun and have just enough concern to get myself outside.

The holler is followed by a boy running toward the house, one hand pressed to the side of his blond head, the other still gripping his stick sword and pumping back and forth as he runs toward me on tireless boy legs. Dirty face, no shirt. Yes, it is Will—so aptly named—and even though he is crying, he isn't sad at all, he is furious.

I am outside for the first time in days and we meet on the porch. He drops the stick at my feet and drops himself into my arms, pouring out an injustice he's been subjected to during a fight with the enemy. Also known as his brother.

"No heads!" he spits out. "That's the rule! Luke did it on purpose!"

I feel a lump starting to form on the side of his head when I peel away his sweaty hand. I look down at his weapon and see the end of it has been expertly sharpened. Probably with a jackknife—all the boys have one of their own, given to them by my brother, Ben, from his camping, hunting, and fishing stash. Someone has wrapped the handle of Will's stick in duct tape for a better grip. I touch the business end with the tip of my finger; it is so sharp, it could spear fish.

"What's this for?" I ask him, holding it up so the point is at eye level.

"For throwing," he answers, looking me in the eye and crossing his arms tightly over his bare chest. "And jabbing."

I've failed my sons. Again. For proof of this, just look at what they've been up to while I'm not paying attention. Owen, who has been such a help these past few weeks, isn't here right now to step in and referee. He's put together a rock band with some high school friends and they're all off writing music somewhere. I should know exactly where, but I don't. Because I haven't been paying attention to that, either.

When I unravel Will's story I find out he didn't yell "Luke squashed my head" but, rather, "Luke threw a squash *at* my head."

The leaves, vines, and manure piles at the edge of our fallow pasture are conspiring together to create log-sized super-squash the boys have each stockpiled in separate caches and are now heaving at each other like Olympic shot-putters. These squash bombs are an anomaly—unplanted volunteers freakishly large because they've grown in their own nutrient-rich greenhouse of sorts—a microclimate in the manure piles along the south side of the barn.

Any other year, I would have noticed them. Any other year, I would have noticed a lot of things.

One of the reasons I am divorcing their father is because he sleeps his way through life. Because he refuses to take any real action against his longtime perpetual melancholy.

This behavior was a shock to me when we got married. I grew up with parents who shared the work of a marriage but who shared the joy, too. It never felt like that was the case between Mr. Wonderful and me. It felt like I got the lion's share of each. But now here I am, all wound up in a melancholy of my own. And what's worse is that there isn't another me to pick up the slack while I take a break from life.

At least in their *Lord of the Flies* moment, the boys have instituted rules. One rule anyway. According to Will, the single decree of pasture war is this: they are not allowed to aim their squash bombs at each other's heads. Any hit to the body is fine, but no head shots.

And my first thought about their conflict is not all that maternal.

Because when I picture my beloved sons raining vegetable bombs down upon each other, the first thing that comes into my mind is not that one of them could have been badly hurt—the sharpened sticks are probably more dangerous than the squash bombs. Nor am I all that perturbed over Luke's obvious lack of fair play. Will may look like a cherub, but I know that he has his own Cain-like tendencies. No, my first thought is that these boys are wasting a potential food source.

Two months in and we are having some success with our

living-off-the-farm efforts, but our money is still dwindling fast. We don't have to buy vegetables at the store, and we have enough extra sweet corn, beans, broccoli, and cauliflower to freeze for the winter. Onions, carrots, and potatoes can be stored in the root cellar in our basement. I make homemade tomato sauce and pizza sauce and salsa, as well as huge batches of basil pesto. Strawberries from the garden mixed with fruit from two ancient mulberry trees in our front yard make great-tasting jam.

I know a bakery that sells day-old bread for half price, and a neighbor down the road has laying chickens and so we are eating a lot of farm-fresh eggs—deviled, fried, scrambled, poached, and hard-boiled. They aren't free at $1.50 a dozen, but they are a cheap source of protein, so we eat a lot of them. So many, in fact, that one night when I put a platter of curried poached eggs and brown rice on the table for dinner, Luke looks first at the entrée and then up at me and says, cave-boy-style, "I want some meat."

"Be patient," I remind him. "That's what Rocky's for."

We've chipped in with friends and bought two piglets. The friends took one and we took the other. Owen has recently turned vegetarian, but I'm still planning that our piglet will grow into a hog and then into enough prepared pork to satisfy those of us who are carnivores. The boys named him Rocky, after the boxing champ. From the glint in Luke's eye, I know exactly what he's thinking. At the mention of our pig, it's not the stocky, bricklike animal with a curly tail and damp snout he sees, but a full-grown ham, propelled around its pen on maple-smoked-bacon legs.

Still, you can't pay an electric bill with bacon and eggs. Or put gas in the car or pay the mortgage on this farm that feels big enough now to choke a turkey vulture. Can you eat turkey vulture? I wonder.

In a fate so purely rendered I'm now certain not only that there is a God, but that She has a crackerjack sense of humor, one of my freelance gigs has morphed into steady work with steady pay. The job? Helping a successful financial planner edit his children's book, *Finding Utopia*. The irony of that title when coupled with our lives is so perfectly timed it shakes me to my agnostic core.

Even with this new source of income we are still short this month. So desperate am I for every penny that I file an insurance claim on the loss of Major. It isn't fair, but it's necessary: a horse's whole life for one month of ours. That check plus the money from selling Pepper will pay our September bills with not a penny left over.

And so here we are, subsisting on eggs, vegetables, day-old bread, and homemade jam day after day, while my boys finish their chores and then decide to have a food fight. They might as well be throwing armloads of rolled coins at each other.

I am no innocent in this predicament, either. I might not be hurling squash bombs at my own family members, but I am letting my melancholy over the end of my marriage, over Major's death, over selling Pepper, over our money problems, over my perfect rural life dissolving in front of my eyes, have its way with me. Grief has pinned me in this chair as tightly as if it were holding Will's pointed stick to the white of my neck.

"Emotional turmoil can interfere with the mom and dad roles even though the husband and wife roles have ended," I read in SMILE. "This is a time when the children need more affection and attention but there is too little of the parents to go around."

Yearning for what I've lost is, I decide right now, an indulgence. An indulgence that's certainly not in the best interest of my sons, but that's also not in the budget.

It's been a month since Major died. My grief over his death will not end this soon, and maybe not ever, but my inaction has to. And when Will and I walk out to the edge of the pasture, I can hardly believe what I see. In less than a month the field of grass that had been bitten to the quick by Major and Pepper is now covered in rambling green. Leaves and vines serpentine everywhere, and hidden underneath, dozens of squashes, some with the heft and density of bowling balls.

"See?" Will says to me, satisfied at my shocked face. "Told you. Bombs."

Luke is in a corner of the pasture, crouching down next to his stash of munitions, a battered lacrosse stick rigged into an arm-powered trebuchet at the ready. He has it loaded and ready to let fly.

Here in Will's stronghold, the remains of shattered squashes are lying at our feet. Seeds, ripened flesh, and crescents of rinds are everywhere. I put my hands under the gigantic leaves, feel around, and wrestle two squash logs from their vines. With one under each arm I walk back toward the house. My sons look at me as if I've finally just gone ahead and lost my mind. Maybe they think I am headed across the road to launch these green torpedoes at their father.

"Dinner," I say instead.

Wordlessly, the young soldiers follow me in. An army, even one noticeably short in stature and including only two troops, still marches on its stomach.

"Even Napoleon Bonaparte had to eat," I yell to them over my shoulder.

The boys will just have to declare a temporary cease-fire. Tonight for dinner we're having squash-crusted pizza out of *The Moosewood Cookbook*. Tomorrow morning for breakfast, eggs Benedict with fried squash medallions in place of the Canadian bacon, and for lunch, some kind of vegetable soup I'll think up, and squash bread with jam. Luke might be having visions of a full ham running around our friends' pigpen, but I'm seeing the dollars on our grocery bill ratcheting down.

"Who is Napoleon Blown Apart?" Will asks, sitting at the kitchen counter watching me cook.

The next morning, Sunday, Owen asks if his rock band can practice in the Quonset hut. All that corrugated metal has got to have some great acoustics, he says. I make a mental note to buy extra bread today on my weekly trip to the bakery. This bakery opens at 9 a.m. on Sundays and everything is half price on this day only. They stay open until they've sold all their wares, which means they almost always close before noon.

For the past month I've been coming here almost every Sunday morning. Their bread is twice as good as store-bought and less than half the price. Although I grew up on my mother's homemade bread, and I know how to bake it, that's a luxury I can't afford. It's actually cheaper to buy this half-price bread than it is to purchase all of the ingredients for my mother's and make it myself.

Even small savings like this one become exponentially more important when you are making enough sandwiches for three hungry boys, yourself, and now extras to fuel the creation of heavy-metal music, too. To quote my bass-guitar-playing son, metal burns a lot more carbs than classic rock or country. And don't even get him started on rap.

With his bass solo jamming its way through the open windows of my minivan, I drive to the bakery. On this particular visit I see a new sign on the counter next to the cash register. In dark-green marker it reads:

ENTER TO WIN!
Annual Biggest Zucchini Contest!

First Prize—$100

Second Prize—$50

Third Prize—$25

For the first time I wonder what the breed or species or ilk or genome the squash bombs in my pasture belong to. Are they, could they be, just maybe, a member of the oft-derided zucchini family?

I try to picture the mystery squash clearly in my mind, without the trappings of combat. I see one, resting under its leafy canopy. It is the shape and texture of zucchini but not the color. Pale green fading almost to white, with darker-green speckles. I wonder how specific the head baker will be in his definition of the word "zucchini."

I see him in the back, kneading some dough. He is average-sized, with a little paunch around the middle, coarse black hair with salt-and-pepper trimmings. White pants, white T-shirt, white apron, hairnet. His hairless forearms look like Popeye's without the tattoo, veined and bulging, and he is focused in on his work. All business.

What, I wonder, will this man think of my squashes?

"Excuse me," I say to the woman behind the counter with the cat-eye glasses, "could you tell me the rules for your zucchini contest?"

Birdlike, she cocks her head at me. "Rules? What do you mean, rules?"

"Oh, you know," I answer innocently. "How many can I enter, when should I bring them in, what do you do with them after, stuff like that."

She waves a bony claw in the air. "As many as you want! We make zucchini bread to sell! Friday, okay? You bring them in Friday."

"And I can really win a hundred dollars?"

"Yes. We put one hundred dollars on a card for you here."

"Oh. You mean it's not cash, but bread and rolls and stuff."

"Yes! Yes! Or cakes! Or cookies! Lucky, lucky winner!"

I think about it. I would prefer the cash, but she is right. Someone, or rather three someones, are going to be lucky winners indeed. At eighty cents a loaf for their day-old homemade bread, first place would pay for a whole year's worth for me and for the boys. That's sandwiches for school lunches, or French toast on weekends, or breadcrumbs for meat loaf, and enough store credit left over for a dozen cookies or even a coffee cake.

Since my regular paycheck doesn't cover us, maybe this is how we're going to make it—by assigning odd little tasks to all our individual needs. Rocky the pig for protein, the garden for vegetables, the SMILE handbook for mental health, the Zen lit for spiritual health, and a crop of volunteer squashes to win our daily bread. I have no idea how I'm going to find the money to finish the remodeling project, but weirder things have happened, I'm sure, even if right now I can't think what they might be.

A bag of sliced seven-grain in each hand, I exit through the automatic door and practically run to the car. I must speak with my troops ASAP and order up some peacetime cooperation.

Once home, I try to explain the maneuver. Owen waves me off, as a carload of boys all dressed in black unloads amplifiers, a drum set, and microphone stands from the trunk of a rusty sedan parked in our driveway.

"Band practice, remember?" he says, laying down a labyrinth of extension cords. I have got to be kidding if I think he has time for *vegetables*.

But I am not kidding, I am totally serious, and Will and Luke take one look at my face and agree to each select the most worthy squash they can find to enter into the contest. From now until Friday morning they'll water their squashes daily, or more often if necessary; they'll pick off any bugs and scare away the crows. They will not, I repeat *not*, use their prize specimens for bombs.

"We're on it," Luke says, saluting sarcastically but still committed to the contest. If he can't outwar his little brother, he'll just outgrow him.

"All right, guys, these squashes are depending on you," I tell them, like the drill sergeant I've become. I *need* that $100 bakery card. "They're like your babies now."

Luke nods his agreement. Will is still thinking about it.

"How about they're like our *prisoners*?" he finally asks.

"Sure, okay, your prisoners. Just treat 'em good."

"They're prisoners, Mom, duh," Will says, as if I were an idiot in the ways of war or he were recalling his treatment at the hands of his brother. Maybe both. "You don't treat prisoners good."

From Napoleon to the Geneva Convention: who knew summer squash came with so many opportunities for edification?

"What about the Geneva Convention?" I ask.

They have never heard of it. Will gets a pass, as I didn't really expect this to be a chapter in his third-grade history book. But Luke just started eighth grade. I would have expected him to know about this important piece of world history and international law by now. Note to self: start attending those school curriculum meetings.

I tell the boys that the Geneva Convention is a worldwide law that countries at war have to obey. We open the big atlas and find the city of Geneva, where the treaties were negotiated and signed. I explain that victors of war still have to care for the wounded and the sick, that they have to treat the imprisoned with respect. They listen intently, as if they're really getting it; then Luke lobs a zinger.

"What about Abu Ghraib? Where was the whole Convention thingy on that?"

Even with restrictive TV privileges, even living on our little farm miles outside of town, even with this exchange occurring when Luke is so busy with school and chores that he has little time to spend with his friends where our country's involvement in Iraq might be discussed, he's got it. And I feel a tenderness toward him, my boy considering war.

Don't forget, I remind myself, *he is also the same boy who aimed an eight-pound squash directly at his little brother's head.*

"That was a war crime," I say. "Those soldiers are going to jail, did you know that? What they did was wrong. Even your enemies deserve your respect. Not your surrender—never, ever that. But your respect."

"Right," comes a brand-new voice on this topic. "Like you do with Dad?"

The band has come inside for a sandwich break, and so Owen has an audience of his peers for this bit of family theater. Throughout my whole zucchini-crop repurposing—from war to (hopefully) wealth building, Owen has been noticeably absent from our efforts. He didn't play war with his brothers, because he was off practicing his cello or his bass guitar. He isn't usually around on most Sunday mornings when I go to the bakery, because he has slept over at some friend's house where they've stayed up late to play and write music. He didn't want to hear my plan for winning the contest, because it is, in his fifteen-year-old world, "so über lame."

War crimes must be a lot more interesting to him than summer-squash contests, because Owen is present with us now. Hands on hips, head cocked to the side, he is all in.

And I want to tell him to mind his own damn business. Even in front of his friends. I want to tell him that his brothers and I are having an important political discussion and that he is off topic. And I would, except that this *is* his business, and this *is* the topic.

The divorce, as much as I've been trying to pretend otherwise, is five people's business—mine, Mr. Wonderful's, and the boys', too. It has stretched beyond what I wanted or expected, out into the world around us. It isn't just happening to me, it is happening to all five of us. *We* are getting divorced.

And amid the anger, the disappointment, the current events, the squash bombs, the grocery bill, and the grief, we are going to have to find a way to live with it.

· · ·

Later that day I settle back into my flowered chair in front of the window. Not for good this time, just for a few quiet minutes. The band has gone home and the boys are in bed. I'm raising three opinionated young men, and discussing life with them wears me out. When they were little, I had all the answers—or if I didn't, I could at least buffalo my way through. Now I sometimes feel like I don't even know the questions.

I bought a Zen book from the library's used-book sale, and when times get tough the author suggests this two-step solution: be aware of your surroundings, and inventory your immediate blessings. This advice from *A Deeper Beauty* sounds easy and harmless enough; I might as well give it a try.

My little farm is almost within sight of the 45th parallel, and this far north the September light late in the day has a golden cast to it. I watch the last of this light drench the slope from the house to the pasture and color my life's present fortunes. A solidly built house. Land I've come to make fertile. Sons who love me and love each other, war games and verbal sparring and gaps of historical knowledge aside.

I take a deep, cleansing breath and ask Someone to *please let us win the contest,* and then I relax back into the safety of my chair. Movement outside in the near dark catches my eye. Tiptoeing past the window in their pajamas are two figures: Will and Luke. They each carry what looks like a rectangular piece of cloth in their hands. What are they up to now?

I walk out onto the front porch and close the screen door very, very quietly. I have no idea where they are going or what they are doing, but I do know that mothers often see the best stuff when our children don't know we're watching them. My two younger boys head for the pasture and slip, like the slim and shaggy-haired shadows of coyotes, behind the barn. In just a few minutes, they retrace their steps and run back toward the house. I press myself flat against the wall by the front door and watch as they run through the mudroom door and then back inside.

I'm not sure if they've seen me here or not, but I wait a few more minutes and hear them both run upstairs and jump back into their beds. Their bedside lights click off, and there is giggling, then whispering, then quiet, then crickets. Right now, two of my immediate blessings are pretty darn obvious.

Full dark comes on quickly, I grab a flashlight and walk out to the pasture. There are lightning bugs twinkling above the vines like low-lying stars, and in two spots on the ground the leaves are disturbed and flattened. I find Will's adopted squash and, nearby, Luke's, too. Each one is still connected to its vine like a beating heart to a vein, but underneath them are two plaid flannel pillow-cases, folded in half. The prisoners, I see, are not only completely safe, but warm and comfy, too.

It's this small kindness that finally cracks me open. "You've *changed*," Mr. Wonderful observed the last time he dropped off the boys.

I am alone now, so I let myself cry, really cry, for the first time since my husband moved out. It's one thing to inventory your blessings; it's another to care for, love, and nurture them in all of the ways they deserve. Money, time, energy, and resolve all feel so finite. So much depends on me now, and I wonder if I am tough enough to shoulder all of it alone. I wonder if I can keep my promise to give them everything by myself.

Last week while Owen was driving with his new learner's permit, a wild turkey flew right into our windshield. We were on a busy four-lane throughway, and I made Owen pull over—not to check for damage to the car but to check for damage to the bird. If the encounter was fatal, maybe we could eat the thing.

There was no carcass in sight, but still, looking at possible roadkill as food is something I never would have done in the early, middle, or even declining years of my marriage. Make a pet of it? Yes. Tape its wing and nurse it back to health with an eyedropper of sugar water? Yes. Pluck it and eat it? Eww.

"If it runs, a Bean will shoot it. If it falls, a Bean will eat it," wrote Carolyn Chute, about her fictional backwoods family. This isn't fiction, though. This is our actual life now. And if it flies into their green minivan's windshield, a Link will pluck it.

I guess Mr. Wonderful is right: I *have* changed. I'm no longer the tree-hugging, agnostic nature lover he married. Now I look at nature in a brand-new way—as something to eat.

With the image of my two sons making their vegetable squashes comfortable on this chilly September night, I hold tight to the knowledge that there is still a bit of goodness in our world. That I find that goodness in the same spot where Major's life unraveled is fitting, I suppose. Abu Ghraib was real and people are suffering and Major is dead and Pepper is gone and I am getting divorced and my children are hurting and we are broke. And I really don't know if I'm tough enough to handle all of it. But inside our sturdy house my three immediate blessings are sleeping the sleep of the innocent. And I am still standing, looking out at our pasture, surrounded, for the time being, by goodness.

. . .

From Monday to Friday Luke and Will care well for their squashes, and it shows. Each soil torpedo has thrived under all the special attention it is receiving and has nearly doubled in length and girth. Their skins have a green cast, but they are mostly white, with a few remaining dark-green speckles. These are not whistling-Dixie, citi-fied, greenhorn, subdivision-garden squashes—oh, no! These are full-scale, all-out, extreme down-a-country-lane squashes, to the max. Whether or not they are zucchini squashes is for Popeye the baker to decide. On Friday morning, he gets his chance.

I've told the boys that they can be late for school today, even though the possibility exists that our squashes might not be zuc-chini and could be disqualified. They refuse to consider this. They refuse to consider anything but victory. And so, wrapped in beach towels and riding on the boys' laps is how the vegetable contes-tants arrive at the bakery.

"Resistance," Luke cheers from the passenger seat, "is futile!"

We enter the bakery single-file, and Will, grinning happily and straining under his burden, announces to no one in particular, "We got two giant zucchinis here!"

With a flourish that would make any magician proud, the boys whip the beach towels off their squashes in unison. There is an intake of breath behind the counter, and three women cus-tomers considering the pastry case turn and stare.

The bakery is silent, except for the sound of industrial-grade mixers coming from the kitchen.

"Mike!" the old woman behind the counter yells, not taking her eyes off the squashes. "Better come out!"

Popeye Mike appears, wiping his hands on the front of his apron. He looks at me, then at the boys; then his dark eyes widen as they come to rest on the two squashes. The boys strain and hold them up for inspection, turning them this way and that. Their pale rinds catch the light and they begin to gleam.

"We'd really like to enter both of these into your contest," I tell him. "We're just not sure that they're zucchinis."

My sons purse their lips and frown, as if I were revealing military secrets. Popeye Mike comes out from around the counter and kneels down in front of both the boys and runs his hands over each of their squashes. He squints, he flicks them with his thumb and forefinger, he bends down and sniffs them.

"May I?" he asks Luke. Luke nods his assent. Popeye needs both hands to grip my middle son's squash and heft it up into the light. He turns it first one way, then another, then hands it back to its owner.

"May I?" he asks Will, who cannot hold his in his arms any longer but is sitting on the floor cross-legged with his squash in his lap. Will nods too, and Popeye Mike repeats his inspection . . . then makes his one-word determination: "Zucchini."

"Yesssss!" Will says, making a fist and bringing it down to rest near his waist like a pendulum.

"Who's your daddy!" Luke shouts.

"These are the rarest of the rare, the white zucchini, and they only appear every seven years," explains Popeye Mike. "They make a zucchini bread like no other."

The old woman behind the counter looks down suspiciously over her cat-eye glasses but smiles in spite of herself. The shoppers forget all about pastries and gather around my sons, admiring their squashes. Popeye Mike is talking now of zucchini muffins and zucchini bread and even mulling the viability of chocolate-frosted zucchini bars.

This is all well and good, but what I want is the store credit. That's what victory means to me.

"Did we win?" I ask.

"Did you win?! Did you win?!" Popeye Mike stands up guffawing, and walks back to the counter. "Look!"

Displayed in a basket on top of the counter is our competition. They are so inconsequential that I haven't even noticed them. A dozen or so dark-green zucchinis no bigger than a small submarine sandwich. Popeye Mike takes our squashes and puts them on the counter next to the basket. They are bigger than all of their competitors combined. They are bigger, by far, than the basket. Popeye Mike holds his paunch and laughs harder.

"You just won first *and* second place! Boys, why don't you pick out a cookie while I settle up with your ma."

On the ride home, the boys' laps are empty, but their hands each hold a giant chocolate-chip cookie. They are a two-man army now, for a few minutes at least, not distant enemies at war with each other, and this makes me feel good.

There was a flaw in our battle plan. If we had entered three zucchinis instead of just two, I'm convinced, we would have won first, second, *and* third place.

Still, for once I—no, *we*—have done something right.

I bungled our finances and allowed my own sadness to infect my sons. Our horses are gone and so is most of our money. But this, this growing of secret-weapon zucchini over a single moon phase with the discipline and hard work of my sons, we've done just about perfectly.

4

October 2005

REAPING MOON

A fool I was to sleep at noon,
And wake when night is chilly
Beneath the comfortless cold moon;
A fool to pluck my rose too soon,
A fool to snap my lily.

My garden-plot I have not kept;
Faded and all-forsaken,
I weep as I have never wept:
Oh it was summer when I slept,
It's winter now I waken.

—CHRISTINA ROSSETTI, "A Daughter of Eve"

September's warm days are gone; there's frost on the pumpkins in the mornings now, and my shoulder is tight to the wheel of the rhythms that dominate our days. It's a restless cold I feel under my jean jacket and work gloves. Work is getting done, though;

and moping, in any form, is a distant memory. But so is the summer garden.

While the boys are at school I come home early from work and can tomatoes and dilly beans, harvest spinach, peas, beets, cauliflower, and heavy armloads of squash. Not the unexpected and freaky squash that won the bakery contest, but the regular varieties I planned for and sowed just before the full planting moon back in May. That feels like someone else's life now, someone else's plan.

At the bus stop one morning, Luke informs me that Einstein believed the concept of time was a fiction, dependent on our silly human need for a past, a present, and a future.

"Don't think about that for too long," Luke warns, climbing the steps of the school bus and about to recede behind the louvered door, "or your head will explode."

With Will in elementary school, Luke in middle school, and Owen in high school this year, for the first time the boys now ride three different school buses, have three different start and end times to their day, and I am wooed by three different PTAs. If anything is going to make my head explode, it's contemplating all of that.

Though I am not, it turns out, exactly PTA material.

The elementary school's parent group is mulling field-trip opportunities when I show up to their meeting, fresh from muddy garden chores and eager to help. I missed the curriculum committee, but I can at least plan a field trip, can't I?

I think of those dozens of sets of idle hands and young backs with willing dispositions, cafeteria-provided snacks, and free transportation. And are you kidding me, of course I have an idea. They can spend the day at the Big Valley and learn how to weed, muck out empty stalls, compost aging horse manure, and shell overgrown beans. They can core tomatoes, blanch broccoli, and trim back perennials. They can *work*. It's perfect!

My obvious excitement at this brilliant use of public-school resources is, surprisingly, not returned by the rest of the parents, and a vote is taken. All in favor of a puppet show say aye, there's a full chorus of ayes, and I never attend another PTA meeting.

While the boys are at school, I stay away, and today mull over Luke's advice about time and know that Einstein must not have been a gardener. He must not have had to put food by for his family for the winter. If he did, he'd know that time is as real as dirt and rain, and in the north you need four good months of it to turn a dime-sized seed into a blue Hubbard squash the size of a Thanksgiving turkey.

If time really is just a fiction, then why do I feel like there's never enough of it?

I snap the blue Hubbard off its frost-wilted vine and carry it downstairs to join its colleagues in the root cellar. Stacked in pyramids in the cool dark like swollen bottles of fine wine are a couple dozen butternut, acorn, and delicata squash. Carrots will stay sweet in the garden until the soil around them takes a hard freeze, but then I'll pull them up, trim their tops, and pack them in cardboard boxes filled with bags of sawdust left over from the stalled remodeling project and store them down here, too.

Last night the boys and I picked all the green beans that grew too large and tough to eat whole, then I spent an hour sliding my thumbnail along their seam and plucking out the seeds. These are much like the dried beans you can buy at the grocery store, but softer and better tasting. They can be sautéed in olive oil for succotash, added to soups, mixed into stir-frys.

In just a few short weeks I've gone from contemplating the

beauty of mythical TV ranches to finding a use for old string beans. Two months ago I fancied myself the Victoria Barkley of the north, striding through my range-riding life. Today I'm sitting on my front porch, big toes poking out of wool socks, shelling beans into a jar. These changes happened so fast, it almost feels like time travel.

And this day speeds by too, just like the others before it, but at four o'clock Owen bursts in the door, the first one home from school, grinning wide, his face flushed with excitement.

"Aberration's got a show!"

His band has been invited to play "a show," he says, this very night. Usually when my sons use terms I don't understand I just give a nod and hone my ears, sure that an understandable meaning will eventually make itself known without my having to reveal my unhipness. And although I gather from his body language that "a show" is something to take pride in, I don't. Not yet, anyway.

"A show" sounds suspiciously like something public. I've been trying so hard to keep us within target range of normal that I really don't want anyone to know that my oldest son, my pride and heir, not only thinks that he is an aberration but aligns himself with a posse who share this worldview and even name their band in honor of it.

You're supposed to feel like an aberration in your teenage years, I gently prompt, when they're here practicing together in the Quonset hut. *That's the point.* It's normal, I assure them. If there's anything at all abnormal about these boy musicians, it's that for a high-school death-metal band, they are actually pretty good.

"What kind of a show?" I boldly ask Owen, who looks at me with what can only be pity.

When I was a teenager, going to a show meant going to see a movie at the movie theater. But in today's teen parlance it means paying a cover charge to go into a basement, a parking lot, a VFW hall, or a farmer's field to hear local bands play. And tonight, just a regular old Wednesday night with school tomorrow, Aberration has been booked to perform at one of these events for the first time.

Owen even pulls a homemade poster out of his backpack with the band's name on it as proof.

"Will you drive us?" he asks. Not "Can I go, Mom?" because he knows me, and knows that letting him go, and letting him stay out late on a school night, won't really be an issue for me where something as important to him as music is concerned. Because he is my oldest, and has plenty of experience to draw upon, he also knows that this is how I mother: it does not even occur to me to say no.

Even though according to the poster they don't go on until 10 p.m., and even though that means they might not get to bed until 1 a.m., and even though Owen has to be at the bus stop by 6:35 tomorrow morning for school, and even though if I agree to drive them Luke and Will are going to be home all alone, and will have to put themselves to bed, it still does not occur to me to say no.

Which son has a better chance of encountering danger? The fifteen-year-old out with his friends onstage at a late-night, coed, teenage rock "show"? Or an eight-year-old and his middle brother, who just turned thirteen, home alone with two loyal dogs, a microwave oven, and homework?

Owen spends hours practicing his bass guitar, he plays the cello in his school orchestra, and he has learned to play keyboard, drums, and acoustic guitar all on his own, without lessons. He wants to be a professional musician. Late nights like this one are a big part of the life of a musician. A hard life, I imagine. And if that's the life my son is dreaming of for himself, he might as well learn that now.

Luke helps us load up the minivan with amplifiers, instruments, drums, microphones, microphone stands, and enough coiled extension cords for the whole band to rappel down Mount McKinley. I put Luke in charge of Will and then drive Aberration to the VFW. We arrive at eight. There are four other bands performing tonight, and as performers themselves, Owen and his band won't get paid, but they will get into the show for free—a bonus, since these boys don't have any money, and I don't have the extra twenty-five dollars it would take to get them all in the door.

"I'll just hang out here with you guys," I say to the band as we unload.

Most of Aberration ignores this, focused as they are on plugging things in, turning things on, adjusting the feedback, but Owen is horrified. He's trying to smile at me, but it comes off as a grimace.

Mom does have her uses—arms strong enough to load and unload equipment, possession of a valid driver's license and a minivan—but right now I'm pretty sure he's feeling jealous of orphans.

"But this is your first gig!" I say, reacting to his expression since he's said nothing. "It's like you were thinking I'd just drop you off and leave or something."

"Huh?" he says, grinning now. "I would think that might be considered *normal.*"

My beloved firstborn is just tickled to death with himself as he says this, and negotiations ensue. He and I eventually agree that

I will make myself scarce until midnight, on the condition that he not guzzle, sip, snort, shoot, smoke, inhale, or otherwise ingest anything I would find objectionable.

"You are not too old to ground!" I warn out my minivan's window as I drive away. Despite my outburst, and the groups of kids turning to see who this crazy woman is, Owen appears visibly relieved.

I call Luke on my cell phone and check in. Everything's fine; they've both finished their homework, the dishes are in the dishwasher, they've got their pajamas on, and they're watching a video, *Princess Mononoke*. No, I don't need to come home.

I've been trying to get Owen to read something besides *Rolling Stone* and *Spin* magazines, and I've got some leverage now, so I head over to the library. I get there just before closing and check out a novel that I actually hope will hold his interest the way his iPod and a sheet of music do.

And I'm just pulling out of the library parking lot at 9:30 when my phone rings.

"Where are you?" a masculine voice on the other end of the line asks.

The only men who ever call me up besides my sons are my father and Mr. Wonderful, and this isn't either of them. At first I think it might be the police and that Owen is in some kind of heavy-metal trouble, but I discard that quick. Because although I can't place the speaker, this is a voice I recognize. Somewhere in the background of the phone call, an engine revs.

"Is that a metaphysical question?" I ask, sarcasm being my default setting these days, especially where men are concerned.

"No," the voice answers neutrally enough, "it's a geographical question."

Ah. Now I connect the voice with its person. This is the builder. Pete. The builder I had to let go back in June for lack of funds. The builder who left all that sawdust a month ago. He's probably calling to see when he can get back to work on the remodel.

I describe my location and the errand at hand in these exact words: "I'm checking out a library book for my head-banging son who is getting ready to go onstage with Aberration at the VFW."

Another man might be confused by such a scenario or at least inquire after more details, but Pete seems genuinely unfazed. I might as well have told him I was planted on my couch, tipping back a Bud Light, watching rebroadcasts of *Deadliest Catch* like all good, self-respecting northern Michiganders did on Wednesday nights.

"Perfect," he says. "I'm right around the corner. I was thinking we could meet for a drink."

Are bars the place where most stalled remodeling projects are discussed? Maybe so. Or is this another kind of invitation? That's a shocking thought and inspires several awkward seconds of dead air. The only sound comes from his end of the line, an engine again, but this time it's idling.

When I can speak, I babble on about what a "show" is and how I might be needed to apply direct pressure to mosh-pit injuries, replace blown amplifier fuses, or at least help coil up extension cords and drive the band members home. But I probably have time for one drink.

And that's how my minivan ends up in a parking lot two blocks from Owen's debut. That's how I end up walking into a dive bar that gets a lot of ink in our local newspaper as being the site of regular cocaine arrests, drunken fights, and domestic violence.

Considering the rules I just laid down for Owen about steering clear of bad influences, does my presence here strike me as the slightest bit hypocritical? Of course not. Is it prudent to go into this bar late at night as an unarmed woman alone? No, it is probably not, but it is the closest bar to the VFW, and they probably have a pool table, so maybe I can even win a few bucks.

And eighteen dollars in my pocket later, in strides Pete. He is wearing black leather motorcycle chaps over his jeans, carrying a leather jacket in one hand and a helmet in the other. So that's what that engine sound was—a motorcycle.

The bar is long and narrow and I am in the back, and so the effect of watching this man who worked on my house almost every day for more than two months walk toward me now is to wonder why I'd never really noticed how broad his shoulders are. So it's true, then: I am still alive.

"Last ride of the season," he says, squeaking onto a bar stool like Clint Eastwood on his *Pale Rider* Appaloosa. Or maybe like Cormac McCarthy's John Grady Cole, outside right now in my minivan, cantering over the pages of that library book on a magnificent but stolen bay.

"I've got another helmet," he says to me, lifting a finger in the bartender's direction. "I'll take you for a ride in the spring if you want."

Aberration will need to be picked up in an hour. My drunken wedding-dress donation caper aside, I normally won't drive if I've had more than a single drink, so tonight I can think only in increments of one hour at a time. That's all I have. That's all I ever have lately, it seems.

Here is a man who thinks in months. A man who knows what he wants whole seasons ahead of time. I must have been able to do that once too, but somewhere along the way I've lost the ability. That motorcycle ride might as well be planned for the next time I orbit the dark side of the moon.

"Maybe," I say. Because after the light-years of time travel into the future that is next spring, "maybe" is really all I've got.

"Morning, Mom!"

Owen actually beats me out of bed the next morning, eager to prove it was a good idea to let him play the show with his band. I'm the one that's a little sluggish, and while I drink my coffee he helps get his brothers some breakfast and even reminds Will not to forget the homework he left on the counter last night.

All three boys are getting ready for school and I let myself relive my hour with Pete. Owen wasn't the only one who had a "first" last night. That was the first time I've been out with a man since Mr. Wonderful moved out. And it hadn't occurred to me until now that although we talked about a lot of things—Harley-Davidson motorcycles and music we like and sport fishing and pool playing—we never once talked about the remodeling project. He didn't even bring it up.

Which seems odd but is just fine with me, because even though I've still got a new bedroom with no trim, a new bathroom with no tile or fixtures, and a new stairway without a handrail, I don't have the money to address any of it.

Soon as it is light out, I'll get my mind off of him and onto the chore of food storage and cut the last heads of broccoli and cauliflower out of the garden, survey everything we've got stored, canned, and frozen now, and just hope there's enough to help us get through the winter.

As the chill walks its worried fingers up my legs, I do know that there is at least one bright spot in the larder. When I came in from the garden last night, I saw the light blinking on our answering machine. Word has arrived that Rocky, a piglet we've raised with friends at their farm in their pigpen, has topped 220 pounds. Soon we'll have ham with our scrambled eggs, stuffed pork loin for dinner instead of stuffed squash, and bacon with our pancakes, bacon with our salads, bacon crumbled into steaming bowls of cheesy cauliflower soup, bacon with our . . . bacon.

This is an approximation of Rocky's weight, because no one put him on a scale; my friends just took a measurement around his baby back ribs and plugged the figure into a mathematical formula to estimate his weight. Two hundred twenty-something pounds is his "on the hoof" weight, and exactly what we were aiming for. Much heavier, and the meat will be too fatty for our liking.

To everything there is a season, and it's time to harvest our hog.

"Today's the day," the telephone message from my friend's husband announces. "You and the boys should come over for the killin'."

The imaginary bacon breeze wafting into my nostrils like a cartoon come-hither finger dissipates immediately and my appetite is in some jeopardy because his statement is not phrased in the form of a question. There will be a killin', and we are expected to be present.

After we bought Rocky and he was settled into his pen down the road, I paid a visit to the Traverse City Public Library to conduct swine research. My friends had never raised pigs before, weren't inclined to read up on how to do it, and so the task of research fell to me.

Turns out, raising a pig for meat is pretty easy as long as you design its living quarters to rival the maximum security at Leavenworth. In all matters of a porcine nature, it's best that "pen" just be considered an abbreviation for "penitentiary."

You wouldn't think that an animal with the silhouette of a basset hound and the shape of a dirigible would excel at Houdini-ish contortions, derring-do, and gravity-defying escapes, but woe to the rookie pig farmer who underestimates *Sus scrofa domesticus*.

Until he topped 140 pounds or so, Rocky's MO was to tunnel under the fence, roll sideways like a greased watermelon, air-paddle his girth up out of the dirt until he was free of the wire, and then it was full speed ahead toward the deep cover dreamed of by fugitives everywhere: the forest. Pigs are the Indy race cars of the livestock world and can work up some serious speed if allowed to bust into the open.

Once they're on the lam, it isn't likely they'll return of their own accord, either. Besides tasting great with a caramelized glaze, pigs have one singular skill: rooting in the ground for food. The woods around my friends' farm teemed with mushrooms, tree bark, fungi, grubs, and apples dropped from long-forgotten trees, so I mused that Rocky was like Henry David Thoreau out there. He went to the woods to live deliberately, to see if he could learn what it had to teach him; then, when it came his time to die, to discover that he had really lived.

Despite his muscular body, Rocky was not a prizefighter like his namesake, after all, but something more sophisticated: a philosopher. At least until my friend's husband and I cornered him against a big stump and lugged him squealing back to his pen. At least until today and his impending "killin'."

I call him back: "I'll be there," I promise.

But as I hang up the phone, a headline in a magazine article from my research pops into my head: "Ask yourself: Can you do the big 'S'?"

I'm pretty sure that capital letter does not stand for "Sissy." I'm pretty sure it actually stands for "Slaughter," and my answer to the question is a great big "No way." I definitely cannot do the big "S" myself. But I can and will be a witness to it. The invitation to this experience also included the boys, though. Should Luke and Will be expected to watch Rocky die, too?

On this I vacillate. Yes, because they helped raise him and are going to help eat him, and his death is a natural part of that process. No, because it will probably be gruesome and will make them sad; maybe so sad that they won't be able to eat him afterward, in which case this whole pig-raising enterprise will be for nothing.

I would normally discuss important parenting dilemmas like this one with their father, and we'd make a decision on the problem together. But lately we have been trying to work out a permanent custody schedule, and there is so much hostility between us that we can't even agree on who will pay for new school shoes. So discussing whether or not they should witness our pig being slaughtered is pretty much out. I decide to completely bypass their father this time and just ask the boys what they think.

"I have some sad news," I say to them, as if this animal we've raised for meat were a beloved old dog. "Today's the day Rocky has to be put down. I'm going and you guys can come with me if you want, or just go to school and it will be over with by the time you get home. It's up to you."

We've just finished breakfast, so maybe my timing is not the very best. There's a pause while this news takes root, then three very different reactions.

"You do know that's murder, right?" Owen the vegetarian says, handing down my indictment and shoving his books into his backpack. I wonder if he is psychic and planned his attire for this particular day, because he's wearing a green T-shirt with a graphic of a yellow baby chick above the words "I AM NOT A NUGGET."

Before I can defend myself, Will chimes in.

"So, like, are you going to cut his head off?"

His tone is disturbingly bloodthirsty, yet, I have to admit, practical, too. How exactly does one kill a pig that weighs as much as a man? I only skimmed that step in my research, and this is the first time I've really thought about the specifics of it. I'm pretty sure we won't cut Rocky's head off, but what is the preferred method? Lethal injection? Sharpshooter? Electrocution?

"I'll go," Luke says, saving me from further contemplation. "But when you call to get me out of school, can you just say I'm sick?"

He explains his request this way: any eighth-grade boy who values his order in the teenage universe does not want his friends to know anything about his family's food-gathering methods if those methods deviate from a grocery store, a grocery cart, and a checkbook. We are deviators.

I make the call and Luke and I arrive at my friend's farm and are greeted by an eerie silence. No squealing, no axe sharpening, no nothing, not even songbirds chirping in their woods. Perhaps I've been too hasty in dismissing Mr. Einstein's view of time, because it does indeed feel like this moment is make-believe. Like a Hitchcock movie just before the crows in the attic attack, just before the killer walks into that wheelchair-bound man's apartment, just before young Mrs. de Winter figures out what is really going on inside that creepy estate.

A gunshot shatters this calculating calm, and then another shot too, or else maybe just an echo.

We walk down the hill to their barn and the pigpen and are greeted by the sight of my friend's tall, broad-shouldered husband with his back to us, standing solid as a battle monument in a town square. His head is bent down toward the pigpen, his arms dangle at his sides, and in his hand is the dark shape of a handgun. Do I see smoke wafting from the barrel, or is that my imagination?

"Sorry we didn't wait," he says when he sees us approach. "I wanted to get it over with."

There's a letdown. I've prepared myself to witness death, and tried to prepare Luke for it, too. I've accepted that it is probably honorable, even, to participate in this final step in the process of growing and raising good healthy food for myself and for my sons. For a second, I almost feel cheated. But only for a second.

"Not a problem," I say after a pause, and now relief that we don't have to witness Rocky's death after all floods through me like blood circulating.

In the pigpen were two dead hogs, snuggled next to each other as if they were napping, each with a single perfect gunshot to the back of the head.

I look over at Luke to see how he's taking the sight of two animals so large and so still. It isn't gruesome exactly, but it is final.

"That's a *lotta* meat," he says, riveted.

A discussion takes place about where and how all that meat will be processed, how much the butchering will cost, and the logistics of getting almost a quarter ton of deadweight hog to the butcher. I can pick which cuts of meat I want, butchering is surprisingly affordable, and the hogs will be loaded into my friend's utility trailer and driven to a butcher shop in the next town.

The meat will be especially tender, because we fed our hogs organic grain and vegetable scraps and supplied plenty of clean well water. But also because Rocky and his cellmate were asleep and fully relaxed when they died. Commercial hog farmers might turn up their noses at the idea that panic in the moments before death, and the adrenaline such panic produces, poison an animal's meat making it tough and bitter tasting, but I do not.

The deed is done, and when we get home I can answer Will's logistical question. No, you don't cut their heads off. You kill a hog with a Smith & Wesson .38.

A week later the butcher calls. Rocky's "on the hoof" weight of 220 is now 104 pounds of packaged meat ready for the ancient chest freezer in our basement. My haul includes the standard cuts of pork you'd find in any grocery store: ham, chops, wieners, sausage, roasts, ribs, and of course bacon—lots and lots of bacon, almost fifteen pounds. But when you raise a whole pig, you also get more mysterious-sounding cuts of meat, like picnic hams, side pork, belly bacon, leaf lard, stew bones, and something called ground shank. These are mostly fatty belly-side versions of their (literally) higher-on-the-hog counterparts.

This month is just full of firsts. I attend my first PTA meeting, Owen plays with his band in front of a live audience, a man on a motorcycle invites me to a biker bar, and my happy family of four enjoys a breakfast of pancakes and belly bacon. With the exception of that PTA meeting, these new experiences have all turned out surprisingly well.

This optimistic mind-set is mine when I look in my freezer and see all that meat, tucked safely away in white butcher paper, just waiting to satisfy our winter appetites. Today the temperature did not get above forty degrees, and when I went outside to pick the last of the green beans the heavy air smelled like snow. It's only October, but the wheel is turning and winter is coming. In years past, I always thought of November through April as ski season, snowman-building season, and holiday-decorating season. This year I'm just trusting it's not going to be hungry season, and I have our vegetable garden and Rocky to thank for that.

Belly bacon cooks up like regular bacon, it just has even more fat. But to learn how to prepare the other cuts of pork when the time comes, I turn to a 1950 edition of *Betty Crocker's Picture Cook Book*, a hand-me-down from my German grandmother, my father's mother, Florence Link. Grandma Link died a few years ago, several months past her hundredth birthday, but oh, the stories of meat preparation she could tell!

In her self-reliant heyday, Grandma Link made blood sausage, head cheese, boiled tongue, and pickled pig's feet as the Depression felled her neighbors and took their farms. Frying up some of our side pork or belly bacon would have been as common to her as flipping a sausage patty is for me.

I open up her cookbook to the section marked "Meat-Stretchers," and I believe that this red binder of culinary secrets is a direct line to her frugal kitchen. Just think of all the savory dinners I'll cook for just pennies a plate!

An important consideration, because though their father and

I have yet to agree on either a custody schedule or whether he will pay any child support, I'm figuring on a best case/worst case scenario: that the boys will spend most of their time with me and that financial support for that will be negligible. I flip through the meat-stretching recipes—Meat Patties with Tomato Sauce, Scotch Scallops, Beef Éclat—when my eyes come to rest on a featured recipe for something called Emergency Steak.

In order to make this dollar-stretching delicacy, the home cook has only to mix together 1 lb. of ground pork, 1 tsp. minced onion, ½ cup milk, 1 tsp. salt, ¼ tsp. pepper, and 1 cup Wheaties cereal. This meat batter is then placed on a lightly greased pan and, in the big finish, "patted into the shape of a T-bone steak. Strips of carrot may be inserted to resemble the bone. Broil, serve hot . . . immediately."

Emergency Steak is not something you'd want to eat luke-warm, I'd wager.

The boys and I are not facing this kind of meat emergency—at least not yet, and hopefully not ever. Mr. Wonderful and I have an appointment with the court social worker to discuss how he is going to support the boys. Regardless of what the court decides about that, I am still going to feed my sons well. The carnivores, the omnivores, and the veggie-vore, too. And I refuse to subject a single shaving of our open-pollinated, lovingly grown heirloom Scarlet Nantes carrots to any meat emergency.

Owen can eat our carrots, and all our other garden veggies, however he wants to, whether raw, cooked, or stir-fried. Luke, Will, and I plan on baked ham, pork chops, and of course, belly bacon.

. . .

"When Mardi sells the house, she'll be in a much better position. Financially at least."

I tuck my wool skirt under my behind with my clammy hand and sit down in the social worker's office. We are at our Friend of the Court appointment, and it took me forever first to find a skirt and then to iron it and I'm a few minutes late. When I arrive, Mr. Wonderful stops talking and looks at me, his mouth bolted down in disappointment.

I've long been a disappointment to him, I think—too stubborn, too opinionated, too much—and with this revelation I feel something new: sympathy. For what he must be going through, for how much he is probably missing the boys, for his own loneliness. Seeing me like this—scraggly, out of breath, mismatched, and late—can't be a real picnic for him, either.

All men surely want a wife they are proud of. He obviously didn't get one.

But Mr. Wonderful keeps right on talking as if I weren't even in the room. It takes me a minute to adjust, but then I understand that, incredibly, he's talking about *selling* our farmhouse. He's laying out his opinion to the social worker on what he thinks is a reasonable fate for our sons, a reasonable fate for our money, and, in a move I didn't anticipate, a reasonable fate for our farmhouse, too. It makes the most sense to cut his losses, he says, and just sell the place off.

I stare at him openly, but I'm too shocked to say anything. This is the first I've heard a word about selling the Big Valley. That would be impossible. Where would the boys and I go?

The four of us leaving our garden and our zucchini patch and Major's memory and our farmhouse is unthinkable, and I feel my brain start to boil. I pay the bills, I feed the dogs, I water the garden, I clean his leftover junk out of the garage, and I climb down into the well pit with a flashlight to jiggle the pump wire when it shorts out. I make sure our boys still have one stable thing in their life: their house.

But half the Big Valley still belongs to him. He's not going to relinquish that half to me just because the boys and I have been caring for it by ourselves for a few months. This is what penetrates my naive Rebecca of Sunnybrook brain stem as I turn to face the bearded social worker.

"But we have an agreement," I say, concentrating hard on keeping my wrath at bay. From my wealth of past experience in conflicts with the opposite sex, I do know that irate women fare poorly in arguments with logical-sounding men.

"Let's take a look at it," the social worker says, his beard bobbing up and down when he speaks, "and we'll just see if it meets the standard guidelines."

Regardless of the agreement that their father and I have worked out, the default arrangement for two working parents who divorce is still for their children to spend one week with one parent, and the next week with the other parent. This arrangement is called "week on, week off." I have overheard mothers at the boys' schools use this term, and it sounded like "weak on, weak off." And I know that I cannot, will not, be weak.

Without my sons I won't even need the farmhouse, because I will die. I will die if I have to be without them for a week, and then another week, and then another. No blood, no guts, and no mess, I will simply sit down again in my flowered chair and cease. Although the mission of the Friend of the Court is to protect children,

I look around this social worker's claustrophobic office and know that I am here for one single, selfish reason: to save my own life.

The Friend of the Court encourages divorcing parents to work out a custody arrangement themselves, and though Mr. Wonderful wanted week on, week off and I wanted him to volunteer for the first manned space mission to Mars, we have managed to compromise. He will have regular "parenting time," but the boys will live mostly with me. This is our agreement, but the social worker still has to put his okay on the schedule.

I unfold the paper and hand it over. The social worker, the Beard, smooths out the creases, reads through it quickly, and then turns to his computer. Typing away, he tells us that we are only one of his nearly six hundred cases and that if all goes well today, we will never meet with him again. That is his goal.

And this is the first thing he's said yet today that I understand. Because I don't belong here, in these clothes, in this room, or with these men. I belong back on the Big Valley, waiting for my kids to come home from school. I belong in the garden, or in the kitchen, opening a package of our own ham, thawing sweet corn, and cooking them a good dinner.

Mr. Wonderful is leaning in his chair, tipping it back, and his arms are crossed behind his head, making his sweatshirt ride up. His pale belly reveals too much and I have to look away, but not before I feel real regret for our sons. What noble boys they are, in spite of their parents' bickering. I wish I were bold enough to kneel down on the floor in my skirt and grab the chair legs and yank his world right out from underneath him.

Is this what a "good mother" thinks about? Probably not. I look over at my husband. He looks calm. Rational. And not at all like he is plotting any such thing against me.

The social worker's computer is loaded with a software program called Prognosticator 19.0, and all he has to do is key in the variables—number and ages of the minor children, income and monthly expenses of the mother, income and monthly expenses of the father, custody schedule—and his computer does the figuring. There is actually an algorithm for lives like ours. Who gets whom, and what, and where, is calculated not by this man's supposed savvy about parent-child relationships, or by the reason for our divorce in the first place, but rather by a mathematical formula.

The printer prints and the social worker hands us copies of paperwork that we are expected to read, agree to, and sign, right here, right now. And I try to read through it, but the text blurs and all I see is: "This case has been calculated with the mother as head of household and having primary physical custody."

No weak on, weak off, not for my sons. They may be spending time at two houses now, but when they say "home," they'll mean the same place they've always called home. They'll mean *my* house. And just as quickly as they appeared, all thoughts of chair tipping evaporate.

Mr. Wonderful is looking at the paper and frowning so hard his eyebrows almost meet up with his bunched-up lips. He leans forward and the front chair legs bump back onto the carpet. Leveled, he flips the paper over, then flips it back again. I look at the paper again too and see the amount of child support he is supposed to pay. It is a lot.

Then the Beard pulls open his desk drawer, reaches inside, grabs two ink pens, and slides them across his desk in a V toward us.

"This is too much," I say, ignoring the pen assigned to me.

"What?" asks the Beard.

"This is too much money."

The Beard looks at Mr. Wonderful and Mr. Wonderful looks at me.

"She's right," Mr. Wonderful says, nodding. "She doesn't need all this. I'm telling you, all she's gotta do is sell the house and everything will be fine."

"This is, ah, highly unusual," the Beard says, after a pause. "We don't recommend deviating from the formula."

Deviating from the formula, I almost shout, has become our modus operandi. Our habit, our practice, our way, practically our religion. But I stay silent on this and instead, say I'll take less. A lot less. A decision that will echo over the cold wood floors, and bounce around our empty refrigerator, and infect my credit rating in the months to come, but one I make in all earnestness now.

I want my husband to be able to recover from this. Emotionally, but financially, too. And what the Prognosticator is suggesting is a fortune by my standards. By Mr. Wonderful's, too. There's no way he can afford to pay me that much, pay his rent on the house across the street, and pay his other bills. I'm the one who wanted the divorce, and so I can't ask him to pay me that much money every month. If I did, he'd go broke for sure.

Plus, I know that if he has to pay me that much money every month, he'll ask for more time with our boys. I do want them to have a relationship with their father. I just don't want to give up even one more minute with them than is absolutely necessary for that to happen.

And maybe this is all my fault. Maybe without me around, he *would* be able to move on, be happy, perk up. Maybe it's *me* that's been bringing him down and not those dipping serotonin levels.

"I'm good with that," Mr. Wonderful says, grabbing the pen.

The fate of the farm will depend on what we can work out

with our lawyers. The property and the farmhouse will have to be appraised. If they're sold, we'll split the proceeds that remain after the mortgage is paid off. If I keep them, I'll have to refinance and get a mortgage in my name only.

"We know a good realtor," Mr. Wonderful says, putting down the pen, slapping his thighs with both hands, then standing up and shaking the social worker's hand. He is still convinced that I'm going to sell the farm. He's wrong.

I stand up, smooth my skirt, and smile at both of these men. I have my boys. *My* boys. I have to grit my teeth just to keep from yelling it out loud.

5

November 2005

FROST MOON

May we all be fortunate enough to have a path shown us by the universe, and may we all have the courage to follow it. Enlightenment need not arrive all at once straddling a bolt of lightning . . . It might come in small packages as moonlight reflected in the frost of a cold November morning.

—DANNY SWICEGOOD, *How We Are Called*

The boys eat cereal for breakfast at the kitchen counter on a chilly Saturday morning, wearing their winter coats over their pajamas. I can see my breath inside our house, and the gas bill reads, "Past Due Amount: $279.00."

I've been so focused on feeding us over the winter that I haven't given enough thought to how we're going to stay warm. We have a perfectly good furnace; I thought we'd just use that—until I saw what heat costs. I should have listened to the Prognosticator.

When I was my sons' ages, heat was never a problem. I remember being so warm as a girl. As if there were a tiny furnace inside of me, generating just the right amount of heat in my body regardless of what the elements were doing outside of it.

There I am, decades ago in my burnt-orange bathing suit, diving off the end of my grandparents' dock, over and over again.

The sun is starting to go down and all the other kids are on shore shivering. My brother and my cousins are trembling inside their beach towels, but mine sits folded on the dock and I don't even feel the cold. The lake is mine.

I put my palms together, point them toward the dark and unknowable center of the earth, and dive. My arms are pale, freckled, stick-thin. But underwater, they are ablaze.

"C'mon, Mard, *right now*. It's time to go up. It's getting dark."

My mother is only momentarily exasperated. She's proud of me, I know, because she was a girl raised among boys too, once. She knows the singular joy of outlasting them. Of outswimming them, of outrunning them, of outthrowing them, and of hitting a baseball so hard they can't catch it.

I pull myself onto the dock, stand up dripping, and my mother leads us on our walk up the steep hill to our grandparents' house. I'm right behind her, pine needles sticking to the undersides of my bare feet. "Warm as bathwater," I say over my shoulder to the shivering boys, my towel draped over my arm.

Soon enough the image is gone and I'm right back to our gas bill. "To Avoid Shutoff Send Payment Immediately." And then the company tagline at the bottom of the bill: "Comfort and Efficiency for $3 a Day!" Only a couple of bucks for heat. That seems completely doable. And yet I have fallen behind even on this.

Our clothes dryer, our hot-water heater, and our ancient furnace all run on natural gas. I've set the furnace at fifty-five degrees; just warm enough to keep the pipes from freezing. We can hang clothes out on the line even in winter and they will eventually dry. I've encouraged the boys to take showers at school after gym class whenever they can. If we need hot water for other things, we can boil it on the electric stove, but we are going to need an alternate source for heat.

Please God, help me think of something.

This should not be an insurmountable problem. Humans have been figuring out ways to keep themselves warm for thousands of years. I am an educated adult woman in possession of a perfectly good journalism degree, and I should be able to figure it out, too.

The three boys put their cereal bowls in the sink, put on their winter gloves, and head for the TV in the family room and Saturday-morning cartoons.

I burn the heat bill in the fireplace and watch the exclamation point turn to ash. Alternatives. I need alternatives and I need them now. The tiny furnace inside of me isn't enough today, and even though my sons don't complain, I know they are cold.

The worst part? It's only the middle of November. Winter hasn't even started yet.

By afternoon the sun is out and the temperature climbs to almost sixty degrees. If you don't like Michigan's weather, the saying goes, just wait a minute. And if I don't like whatever problem is confronting me, I can just wait a minute for that to change, too. A new one is bound to be along shortly.

This is an unusually warm day for this late in the season, but not unheard of, and so I know it's not an answer to my prayer, it's just a temporary reprieve. Still, I might as well take advantage.

I open up all of the windows in the house, because it is actually warmer outside than it is inside. The boys must be getting used to me doing things that go against convention, because while they watch me, and Will even runs to help, they don't bother to comment.

I hear Will's feet pound up the stairs and then the sound of the ancient double-hung windows creaking open in the upstairs bedrooms.

"Mom! There's a butterfly stuck in here!" he yells from his room.

"Open the screen and let it out," I answer back, without even thinking.

I have this sudden image then of my youngest son tumbling out of his second-story bedroom window and falling to the ground while an oblivious yellow butterfly pulses upward, and I'm taking the stairs two at a time. I arrive in Will's room just in time to see a dusty brown moth, the kind that eats sweaters, escape out of the corner of the window where he's loosened the screen just an inch.

"I saved it," he says, smiling.

Another catastrophe averted.

I never used to worry like this. Now, I do. Now, I worry about the boys getting hurt, and about how we are going to eat, how we are going to pay our bills, how we are going to keep warm for the next five months.

Tonight it's sure to get cold again, and sleet is in the forecast. You wouldn't know it by looking out the window, but the deep freeze is out there, gathering strength. The second the sun goes down, it will get cold again, and it makes me tired just thinking about it. It's difficult to do anything—play a game of cards, do laundry, make dinner—wrapped in a blanket.

But it's the weekend and tonight I don't want to worry.

Tonight, a Saturday, a family night with nothing planned, I'd like to do something fun with the boys. Something to take my mind off winter. Like, say, a campfire.

For a century-old house, our place has an uncharacteristically open floor plan. The kitchen, dining room, and living room are all one large rectangle with a big fireplace between the dining room and the living room. The downside of all this openness is that it makes the house difficult to heat. The upside is that there's plenty of space in front of the fireplace for three boys to sit cross-legged and roast marshmallows.

"Let's do an indoor campfire," I suggest.

"That's cool," says Owen, managing to stand and slouch at the same time, his arms crossed over his chest in the teenaged lean.

"Then I call chopping the wood!" Luke says.

Of all of us, he is the best with tools. They fit in his slender hands easily, and with an innate proficiency he knows exactly how to use them. Not just a hammer and a handsaw, but wrenches, chisels, Vise-Grips, and pliers, too. Even the hatchet.

This last tool is out in the shop, a rustic room off the north end of our Quonset-hut garage that used to function as Mr. Wonderful's office, workshop, and escape hatch. It has a pockmarked cement floor, but the walls and ceiling are drywalled, it's well lit, and separated from the rest of the garage by an old sliding glass door. For heat, it has a small woodstove.

Luke has recently claimed this space as his. It used to be referred to as "Dad's shop," then as "the shop," and now it's called "Luke's shop." He has made swords, spears, and shields here. He has sharpened the arrows he's made for his bow here, spent hours reading, carving, cutting, nailing, and chopping things out here, too.

Above the woodstove, my middle son has taped a Ralph Waldo Emerson quote: "To the illuminated mind the whole world burns and sparkles with light."

Luke and I head out to his shop together and he finds the hatchet hanging in its spot on the pegboard. My dad keeps his tools on a similar pegboard that hangs on the wall in his shop. My grandfathers both kept their tools on pegboards in their shops, and it brings me some satisfaction to see that Luke does this, too. I cannot teach him all the man skills he needs to know, but at least some of them are being filtered down from the men in my family. He could do no better than to grow into men like my dad and my grandfathers.

Inside this small room, I exhale and realize I have been holding my breath. I don't come out here often. The specter of Mr. Wonderful is still here, and I can smell him. Acidic sweat, the kind that rots the armpits and necklines of T-shirts. Old Spice deodorant, spearmint Altoids. And something else I recognize but try to ignore.

"Not good," Luke says, running his finger across the blade of the hatchet. The business end is caked with dirt and rust. It probably hasn't been used since we all went camping together as a family at Leelanau State Park two summers ago. Somebody put it away without cleaning it first. It wouldn't cut a dry leaf in this state, let alone logs for the fireplace.

"Maybe the whetstone is still around here somewhere," I suggest.

So we look for it. I pull open the overhead cabinets that are too high for him to reach and he looks in the workbench. There are plenty of places it could be. Doors and drawers creak in complaint as we go through the room pulling and banging. Luke pauses and I notice him looking way back into the dark recesses of a far drawer.

"Check this out," he says, holding up a wooden pipe almost as long as his forearm. It has a big bowl on the end and is painted yellow, blue, and red. The painted finish is swirled, as if someone mixed three primary colors of paint together and then dipped the pipe in. Probably while sitar music played in the background.

A cloud of the smell I've been trying to ignore floats out of the drawer in an invisible but unwelcome mass.

"Go back outside," I tell Luke.

The night my marriage ended I was working as a waitress and had just brought home the most I'd ever earned in tips in a single shift: $112. Night editing, writing, or reporting jobs are nonexistent in a small town like ours, and I didn't want my sons in day care, so I got a waitress job at a local tavern. On the busiest nights, I wouldn't get home until after midnight.

I wore a black waitress apron with two horizontal pockets tied around my hips. One pocket was for pens and my order pad and the other was for my tips. Although I usually took the apron off when I clocked out, on this night I left it on while I drove home. I wanted to feel the weight of all that money pressing down against my lap.

What would we use it for? Something fun for the boys, like a trip to the movies, maybe? A special treat from the grocery store— shrimp or salmon steaks? Or something practical, like putting it in the savings account?

I imagined the look on Mr. Wonderful's face when I showed him my big handful of cash. How proud he'd be. It was mostly one-dollar bills—"the Michigan bankroll," the waitresses I worked with called our end-of-the-night cash.

When I pulled into the driveway the light was still on in the shop. I looked at the clock on my dashboard: 1:35 a.m. He must have left the light on. He was always leaving lights on. He left doors ajar, cars running, shoes untied, and gates opened, too. He just spaced out, I guess, always meaning to get to everything later.

I opened the shop door and reached my hand in to turn the light off and there was my husband, sitting in this very spot, his back to the door and to me. He tossed a hasty look over his shoulder and then started grabbing at something. I didn't remember how glazed his eyes looked until later. I guess he didn't hear me pull in, didn't see my headlights, didn't hear the car door close.

"Check this out," I said, reaching my hand into my money pocket.

He didn't turn around, but just kept frantically grabbing at something on the workbench. His back was blocking my view, so I couldn't see what it was, but something was off. He was acting weird. Guilty.

"Look how much I made tonight," I said again, a little cautiously this time, walking up behind him and looking over his shoulder.

And that's when I saw what he'd been trying so hard to hide. On his lap was a plastic bag. When I walked in, he'd been trying to brush everything into the bag before I could see what he was doing.

I'm no antidrug crusader. I'd smoked my share of joints in college and at parties, but I mostly put that behind me when we had a family. He promised he would, too.

"I can't believe you!" I yelled, before slamming the shop door so hard it bounced right back open as I hurried into the house to check on the boys.

This is not my life, I remember thinking. *This is not my marriage. This is not me.*

I look out the window of the shop now and see Owen, Luke, and Will breaking up sticks for our campfire. Owen and Will are smiling, but Luke is not. I make a small fire in the shop's woodstove, toss the painted pipe in, shut the door, open the flue all the way, and listen to the burn.

I find the whetstone in another drawer, spit on it, and make circles with the flat side against the blade. It's just surface rust and it falls away like dust. I head for the woodpile. The boys stop what they are doing and watch me go to town on a couple of logs. Chips of wood fly for several minutes, and the boys take a couple quick steps back but say nothing.

I am not a delicate woman. I am tall and strong. My arms are still freckled like they were when I was a young girl, but they're not stick-thin anymore. I have good muscle, and my middle son didn't get his facility with tools from his father, he got that from me.

"Lumberjack Mom!" Luke cheers, half-smiling now.

His fist is raised and his foot is perched on a big stump. Will copies his brother's stance and repeats the pronouncement.

Behind them, a corkscrew of smoke curls up from the woodstove's chimney. I hack on, and soon sweat from all that chopping makes the hatchet slippery in my hand.

"Here," I say, wiping the rubber handle on my jeans and passing it to Luke. "Careful, it's pretty sharp."

With measured strokes far more efficient than the ones produced by my hacking tantrum, Luke cuts up the kindling, then moves on to the larger pieces. It's late afternoon, and in an hour the sky turns darker and the sleet the weather forecast promised starts coming down, but he's cut up quite a bit of firewood. Enough to fill Will's outstretched arms and Owen's, too. Enough, at least, for our indoor campfire.

You can tell just by looking at it that the fireplace in our house wasn't an afterthought, but was built at the same time the house was. That it is part of the original design. The opening is wider and taller than that of any fireplace I can remember seeing in anyone else's house. The interior bricks that line the sooty cavity are old and chipped and carbonized black with a century's worth of fires. These bricks are big too, closer to the size of a cement block than to a regular brick.

The deed on our farmhouse reads, "Year built: 1900, + or −," and I can picture a circa-1900 family gathered around it before the glass doors or the decorative green-tile surround were added. In my mind, this family would be stirring something aromatic bubbling inside a cast-iron stewpot, warming their hands, drying their darned-over wool socks, and maybe their hand-knit mittens, too.

I cannot picture them roasting marshmallows here, however. Even if marshmallows were invented and readily available to farm families in the Midwest's northern hinterlands at the turn of the century, I'd like to think that the early inhabitants of my house would have known better.

Because as it turns out, building a great big fire in the fireplace and suggesting to the kids that they roast marshmallows over it is not the best idea I've ever had.

I've pulled my chair near the fireplace so I can watch my sons and so I can pass out the marshmallows. Owen does okay, because he is a perfectionist and slowly turns his single marshmallow until it is a yummy gold. He waits until it cools, then eats it straight from the stick in one bite. But Will is short on patience and long on sugar craving, and his fingertips are burnt. Luke has holes in his jeans from sparks popping out of the fireplace and landing on his pant legs.

Every one of our roasting sticks is toast, and those big fire-bricks I was so proud of are now overlaid with strings of scorched marshmallow fluff.

There's also the smell. What comes out of the bag when you tear open a fresh package of marshmallows may be a puff of air that smells remarkably like sunshine. And even burnt marshmallows may smell fine and dandy when you're sitting around a bonfire outside under an evening sky.

But inside the house, burnt marshmallows smell like a chemical plant fire. Sulfur and burning hair mixed with flaming cotton candy. Be advised also that this kind of scorched-sugar snafu is going to set off your smoke detectors. Which will then, in turn, completely wreck any ambience you tried to create for yourself and your sons by building the fire in the first place.

"Mobe, an I aff a ass a ilk?" Will is standing in front of me, his fingers are stuck to his burnt-black roasting stick with marshmallow goo, his lips are moving around a glob of more marshmallow goo, and his freckled face is smeared with ashes and what can only be tears. Between the shrieking smoke detector and the sugar glue in his mouth, it takes me a minute to realize that he's just said, "Mom, can I have a glass of milk?"

I look around at my boys and feel their burns and see the black streaks of char on their faces and smell the marshmallow goo all over everything and mentally take down the score. *Happy family activity—zero,* I think to myself. *Powers that be—one.* No, scratch that. We're out of milk. *Powers that be—two.*

"Owen, please go upstairs and take the battery out of the smoke detector. Get a chair or something to stand on. Luke, get your brother a glass of water—honey, we're out of milk—don't make that face. You do *not* hate water. No one hates water. Hold it, everyone. Show me your hands."

They line up like a trio of singed nesting dolls and flash me their palms. Owen's hands have a few black streaks, but Luke's and Will's hands are covered with ashes from their burnt roasting sticks, there's melted marshmallow layered on top of the ashes, then dog hair and wood chips and just plain dirt stuck to that.

Will reaches into the front pocket of his jeans with a fuzzy paw, pulls out a raw marshmallow dredged with pocket lint, and pops it into his mouth.

Then, small, medium, and large, they file past me, heads down, hands up, heading toward soap and water like a three-pronged human dowsing rod. Owen sprints upstairs and the smoke detector's wailing finally ceases.

While the other two are scrubbing themselves, I consider how to clean the fireplace. Even though the fire is out, the bricks are still so hot that heat radiates out from them in translucent waves. Put down a pat of butter and you really could fry an egg.

It's evening now, colder and windier outside, but the living room faces straight west, and there's a little of the setting sun breaking through the sleet, reflecting off the undulating heat, and making the hardwood floors look, if I squint, like overheated desert sand. But this is no mirage. The living room, the dining room, the whole downstairs isn't just warm, it's almost hot.

I check the outdoor thermometer at the kitchen window. Forty-five degrees. I check the thermostat on the living-room wall. Seventy-one degrees. I am a total moron.

That's why the farmers who built this house put in such a big fireplace. Not to cook over, not to dry socks and mittens in front of, and certainly not for ambience, which they could probably give a rip about in the middle of a Michigan winter. No, they made that fireplace big enough to heat this place.

This is so obvious in retrospect that I feel as dumb as a bag of hammers for not understanding the real function of this ancient hearth.

I got your gas bill, MichCon. I got your gas bill right here.

"There's one!" Luke says from the backseat.

We pull over to the side of the road, Luke jumps out, clicks open the minivan's back hatch, grabs the log he spotted from the window with two hands, and tosses it in. He's back inside smirking at Will and we're under way in less than ten seconds. Up front, Owen has disappeared into his iPod headphones.

"That's six for me and only two for you," Luke says to Will, clicking his seat belt back into place in one smooth motion as we accelerate into traffic. Safety first.

"So?" This has become Will's standard response to his brothers' relentless one-upping. In a year this will turn into "And I care because . . . ?" But for now he sticks to this single-word defense. It usually works. Not much you can do to escalate your own perceived awesomeness when it's received by your little brother with only a sigh, a bored sideways look, and a "So?"

I file this realization away for future use. Yes, I am the kind of woman who is not above using juvenile tactics in adult conflicts. Nor am I above driving around our township in search of firewood that has fallen off someone else's truck. And having my children get out of the minivan to retrieve it. That's right, I will stoop that low. I am a stooper.

"Hey, Bickersons. Quit yakking and watch for wood," I tell them, turning down a forested and potholed side road sure to have something for us. I call this recently devised family bonding activity "Watching for Wood."

The day after the marshmallow fire, the boys and I spent the afternoon cutting up wood for the fireplace from our own property. We should have been doing this all summer, and I'm not sure how much wood we can amass before the snow flies, but we're going to make a run at gathering as much as we can.

I hauled dead trees and downed branches up the hill from the valley, piled them next to the shop, and then the boys used various techniques to hack them into pieces that would fit inside our fireplace. Sometimes this involved the hatchet, but sometimes it just involved leaning the branch or rotted tree trunk up against the cement foundation of the Quonset hut, climbing up and standing on it, then bouncing up and down until it broke into an approximation of the proper size.

Kindling could be broken up by hand, snapped in half over a knee, or cut up with a couple swipes of the handsaw.

This woodcutting went on for several afternoons. The boys would get off the school bus at the end of our driveway, run inside to hang up their jackets and put away their lunch boxes, then come back outside and go straight into Paul Bunyan Jr. mode.

With the industry shown in these after-school woodcutting sessions, it was only a couple of weeks before we ran out of dead trees small enough to cut up with a hatchet and a handsaw. I don't have a chain saw—and I don't want one, either. There actually are a few things that I'm truly afraid of, and a chain saw is one of them.

Large, hairy spiders are another, and I've faced my share of those since we started carrying all this wood through the door and into the house. These arachnid dinosaurs are called wolf spiders and they are horror-flick big, NASCAR fast, and with their hairy legs they twang whatever chord connects my modern brain with its prehistoric cortex. If one gets on me, my fifty-yard dash breaks the sound barrier. I know this because of the silent scream that exits my mouth mid-run.

I can face these spiders if I have to, but I am not willing to face a bloody stump at the end of my wrist. And so, by chain saw–fearing necessity and after exhausting what we can cut with a handsaw, the boys and I take to driving around our township Watching for Wood.

"Pull over!" Will says from his seat directly behind me. He is already unbuckled and sliding open the van door before I've come to a full stop. In my rearview mirror I see his stocky little legs pumping, his bare hands balled into fists and urging him forward like pistons as he runs toward a whole bunch of logs scattered alongside the road. There must be fifteen or twenty of them. Pretty logs, too. Seasoned and split and fireplace ready.

Luke looks over his shoulder and out the back window. "Whoa," he says, impressed with his little brother's score in spite of himself. "The mother lode."

We are stopped on a curve in the road. A curve that must have been too much arc for at least one truck that came through here recently, overloaded with firewood.

"Unbuckle," I tell Luke. "He can't carry all that by himself. Owen, you too."

So far on today's excursion, Owen has been incommunicado, his iPod functioning much like an invisibility cloak.

"What about you?" Owen asks.

Good question. What about me? And soon all four of us are stooping over the stray logs like a murder of crows at a fresh road-kill banquet. I guess I am no longer above jumping out of the van myself and picking up unclaimed firewood. I guess I am not too proud to log-pick after all.

For a moment then I see my family as a stranger driving past might see us through his car window. We are a tall, blond woman in a thin pink Goodwill sweatshirt that bears the slogan "Barbie Dumped Ken" in white stitched-on script. The dark roots in her hair have grown out too far—poverty or carelessness or both, but certainly not a fashion trend.

She loads her arms up with firewood, stacks it high until she's holding the top log in place with her chin. Her eyes are wide; the whites big like a scared dog. This drive-by stranger couldn't know that she's scanning the top log for wolf spiders. But they couldn't miss seeing that she is accompanied by three boys.

The smallest boy has a runny nose and his coat is unzipped. He has to run to keep up with the woman, which he does. This is an almost impossible task, since he is little and since he carries a big log under each arm, but somehow he manages.

The middle boy stays back at the pile and loads logs into the outstretched arms of the biggest boy. This middle boy is wearing a black hat, black T-shirt, and black gloves with holes in some of the fingers. There's a quilted camouflage vest, too big for him, snapped up over the T-shirt. He's thin enough to be called skinny, and yet there are wiry muscles in his bare arms.

Once the biggest boy has taken on the largest load of logs, he walks with purpose toward the minivan, chin up, an intense gaze focused straight ahead. He's appropriated all the accoutrements of a teenager: longish hair, acne, braces, an iPod, and an aura of mortification, imprisoned as he is by his present company.

One by one this foursome heaves their load into the back of a minivan, the biggest boy taking the time to steal a look around before he disappears inside. The woman and the little boy follow, but the middle boy adjusts the wood, shuts the van's rear door, and is the last one to pull his own door closed. Then these vagabonds drive away, spewing gravel from bald back tires.

This is us. This is what we look like.

There is an old saying favored by people who live in cold climates and deem wood the superior heating source over all the others—fuel oil, electric, propane, even natural gas—because it is the only one of these that heats you twice: once when you cut it and again when you burn it.

This is a truism even when you don't actually cut the wood yourself. I know this because my face is flushed hot and I'm all heated up inside just thinking about us there, out in the open, on the side of the road.

6

December 2005

LONG NIGHTS MOON

. . . On some hill of despair
the bonfire
you kindle can light the great sky—
though it's true, of course, to make it burn
you have to throw yourself in . . .

—GALWAY KINNELL, "Another Night in the Ruins"

I just don't know how you do it," my mother says from the other end of the telephone, from the other end of the solar system.

This is my opening. This is my chance to tell her how broke we are and how scared I am. My chance to tell her that the house is so cold in the mornings now when I wake the boys up for school that there is ice on the insides of their bedroom windows.

My chance to tell her that even though I've put plastic over every creaking pane to keep the wind from rattling through, this ice is still advancing. It's growing day by day like some rare and frosty algae able to thrive, so very unlike us mere humans, even this far north.

This is my chance to tell her that our refrigerator is always close to empty and that we're quickly going through our pig and what I've been able to freeze from the garden.

This is my chance to say that I'm not doing it at all, Mom. Not even close.

This is my chance to ask for help.

"We're good, we're fine," I hear myself lie. "But—and pardon my French—the laundry is kicking my ass."

We both laugh at this shared domestic foible. Three active boys in the country can generate black wood-char stains and sweat-soaked socks that, if you're not careful, will burn the motor right out of the Maytag you received two decades ago as a wedding present.

Still, laundry is a safe topic. A constant struggle fought by women the world over, but one no more dire than dirty floors or dusty furniture.

"You could have the boys help you with that," she chides. "You don't always have to do everything yourself."

Yes I do. If there was a mantra in my childhood it was a single word: "accountability." Links might not be flashy, might not be trendy, might drive used cars and wear last year's coats and choose economy over luxury at every opportunity, but Links keep their promises. They show up on time, do their homework, come prepared, get the job done right, and don't complain. Links do not default on their duty, whether it's taking the rag your father hands you on a Saturday morning and rubbing every speck of road tar off his brown Oldsmobile's grille or keeping your adult life solvent. And I am a Link—even marriage didn't change that.

I wanted this house when we could have stayed put in the little bi-level we could afford. I wanted three kids when we could have stopped at two. I wanted the divorce. Me. I made this bed and I'll either lie in it or die in it, but I won't ask anyone for help.

My mother cannot fathom my life now, anyway. Partly because she has no experience with this kind of instability, but mostly because I won't let her.

Laundry, though, is something we have in common. This was one of my chores as a girl. Not washing it—my mother always did that—but folding it and separating it into piles so my brother, Ben, could carry it upstairs.

After school I'd sit on our yellow beanbag chair in the family room, fold the laundry warm from the dryer, and watch reruns of *I Love Lucy*. Sometimes my mother would set up the ironing board for the sheets and pillowcases and my dad's shirts and watch the show with me while she ironed.

We worked together on the chore back then, so it's no surprise that she's reminding me, now that I am a mother too, that I don't have to do it all by myself.

"I know," I say. "You're right."

I don't tell her how much the boys already do help me. I don't tell her they help me gather and chop firewood; that Owen and Luke help build fires in the fireplace; that the boys are the ones who hold the plastic tight to their bedroom windows while I seal it to the wood-frame moldings with my hair dryer, trying to contain the ice.

I don't tell her Owen helps by carrying armloads of squash up from the basement when he would rather be with his friends playing music, or that he researches cheap vegetarian recipes on the Internet and often helps me prepare them, too.

I don't tell her that all three boys help me just by not complaining. Not about their school clothes purchased from the same place I abandoned my wedding dress—Goodwill; not about running out of lunch money in line at the school cafeteria; not about wearing hand-me-down shoes from a friend who also has boys; not about sleeping every night under a pile of mismatched blankets because the thin comforters they picked out to match their rooms a year ago aren't warm enough now.

I don't tell her that my sons exhibit none of the misbehavior and arguing common to most boys and most brothers, because they don't have the time to argue with me or the energy to fight with each other.

I don't tell her that I don't know how I am going to buy Christmas presents for my sons and for the rest of my family or pay the mortgage this month—the mortgage on the house that she and my father both urged me to sell. I don't tell her that the $3,000 they loaned me to pay my attorney isn't enough, that I've already burned through every penny of it and now owe hundreds more, and that the billable hours continue to accumulate, because the divorce hearing isn't until March.

I don't tell her that I still dream about Major most nights and wake up when I think I hear brakes screeching and a horse screaming, only to find that this nightmare, while real, is months old, and our house is actually quiet and dark, and my barn is empty and cold.

I don't tell her that her daughter is the kind of woman who misses a horse she owned for two years more than she misses a man she was married to for almost twenty.

"What do you and the boys want for Christmas?" she asks.

"They could use electric blankets," I say, "and flannel pajamas."

We talk for a few more minutes. Most of our conversations don't last long, because she is a doer, not a talker, and doesn't like to waste time on the phone. We make plans to celebrate a family Christmas together at my parents' house before the actual holiday, so that Ben, who is also divorced, and his daughter, who lives with her mother, can be there with us, too.

I don't tell her what I want for Christmas, because even my parents, as capable and loving and solid as they are, can't fix what I've got going on here with a present. With a hundred presents— even ones beautifully wrapped by my mother.

Christmas Day falls on a Sunday, but we drive down the Wednesday before and spend one night. Ben greets me at the doorway, and I hug him hard. There is a tall birch branch in my parents' dining room that my mother cut, spray-painted, and decorated with a partridge made out of real feathers sitting in the center of it surrounded by twinkling lights. It is lovely and looks like something out of a magazine.

In the family room, the same room where I once watched Lucy laugh her way through motherhood and wifehood and figured that this would be what my adult life would be like one day, is a traditional tree decorated with woodland ornaments and encircled at the base with presents wrapped in gold paper and decorated with sparkling silver ribbons. Hanging above the fireplace there's a colorful felt banner that my mother sewed of a partridge sitting on a three-dimensional wreath made of stitched felt pears and leaves.

There's a fire in the fireplace. The house smells like turkey dinner and pie, and my mouth waters.

The next afternoon the boys get electric blankets and new pajamas and generous donations to their college stock accounts. As they're opening their presents, my mother smiles conspiratorially at me, reaches behind the Christmas tree, and brings out a cardboard box so large she can barely carry it. My dad is grinning, so he must know what it is, too. The box is open at the top, but a huge silver bow glistens there, obscuring what's inside until my mother sets it down right in front of me and I peer inside.

I see two large boxes of laundry detergent, the expensive brand, along with packages of paper towels, napkins, dish soap, dishwasher soap, colorful dishrags and dish towels that match my kitchen.

My mother sits across from me, her hands in her lap, looking pleased with herself for thinking up this practical gift that is also a reminder of our shared role in life as mothers, of our recent telephone conversation, and maybe, though this could be reaching, of my efforts to clean out my life.

Because I've told her that dirt is my biggest problem, she believes me. Not only believes me, but comes up with the supplies to solve it, at least temporarily. And even presents these supplies to me wrapped, literally, with a bow. I laugh and say thank you to my parents and really mean it. Even though it will not scrub the worry from my mind.

Because while the boys and I are here at my parents' visiting, a real-estate appraiser is creeping around the outside of our house and around our property, taking notes and making measurements. His report on the dollar value of the Big Valley will seal the financial part of the divorce.

"Keep your dobbers up!" my dad tells me, after all the presents are opened and we are packing up. He hugs first the boys and then me goodbye. I hug him back for a long time, and my mother, too. The boys will sleep warm tonight back at home, and will at least have clean pajamas, clean sheets, a clean house. All because of the kindness of my parents.

As the boys and I get situated in the minivan, my parents stand in their driveway, married now almost fifty years but still with their arms around each other's waists. My mother likes to say that the first time she saw my father, from a second-floor window of her sorority house, she said to her roommate, "That's the man I'm going to marry." I can't remember having any such moment with Mr. Wonderful, and so her story has always sounded to me like something out of a fairy tale. As I look at my parents now, though, standing there smiling and so tight together, it feels real.

What, I wonder, might they be able to do for us if I could bear to tell them the truth?

We won't ever know, because I plaster a smile on my face, and the boys and the dogs and I drive away from the warm house I grew up in, away from my parents' tidy subdivision, away from Country Estates, and I aim the van for home. The Big Valley, and our messy lives, await.

The next morning, the day before Christmas Eve, the boys and I embark on a housecleaning adventure. This is a hazardous trek that takes us deep into the long-unexplored wilderness underneath living-room furniture and behind large appliances. It is an excursion that provides us with the rare opportunity to see things previously unimagined by the human mind: half a dusty cinnamon roll, pebbles of moldy dog kibble, and a faded and wrinkled copy of *Rolling Stone* magazine with Britney Spears in her underwear on the cover.

Without shame or embarrassment Will admits to ditching the cinnamon roll. He says he ate half, discovered the raisins, got grossed out, knows how I feel about wasting food, and so hid the evidence of said waste under the couch. Good enough.

But when I wave the crumpled magazine in the air, daring someone to claim it, the suspects all seize up. No one will cop to stashing Britney in the same place half-eaten cinnamon rolls go to die, and there's nothing to do but continue onward and scrub some more.

The only actual wildlife we find on this slog through our increasingly cleaner house is small game that's already dead. A mouse is spread-eagled, dried flat and preserved like snakeskin on the coils behind our refrigerator. Luke is the only one who can stomach prying it off.

"Someone finally built a better mousetrap," he says. "It's called a refrigerator."

I stand on a chair and wash walls, then dispatch the rest of the wet jobs—toilet scrubbing, sink scrubbing, mopping, mirrors—and the boys hunt down the dry ones: dusting, rug shaking, and vacuuming. Together we clean the grime from every doorknob, light switch, and stair railing. I do laundry with my newly gifted box of detergent while they clean their rooms.

Housework is not my best skill, and so this ceiling-to-floor scrubbing is long overdue. It makes the place smell great, though, like a pine forest, but it also accomplishes something else. There's now a big empty corner across from the fireplace and next to our still-unfinished stairway without a single molecule of dust, cob-

webs, or dog slobber anywhere. This corner is close to an electrical
outlet, which is also clean, and bordered by pale yellow walls I just
scrubbed. I stand back and look at it, filling the space with my
mind.

I see tiny colored lights, I see tinsel, I see ornaments. Because
this is where we would usually have put up our Christmas tree by
now.

The realization makes tears shoot straight from my eyes like
ammonia from a spray bottle and burn just as bad. Christmas is
in two days, and this is the first time I've even thought about a
tree. The boys must have wondered why we don't have one up yet,
especially after seeing the spectacular one at their grandparents'
house, but they haven't asked me about it. Not once.

I can't believe I'm crying over this, but I am. And these tears
say, *I am a failure.* A failure at life, a failure at single motherhood,
and, maybe worst of all, at least right now, a failure at Christmas.

I can't replicate the mythic Christmas trees of my childhood, or, now that I really think about it, of *their* childhoods,
either.

There's no stopping my pity party now, and the tears turn
to sobs. I don't have the money to buy a great big tree, or the
strength or sharp saw to cut one down myself. Which is a moot
point since we don't have much to decorate one with, anyway.
When we divided up our winter things, Mr. Wonderful got half
our ornaments. And our Christmas tree stand. At least, I think
that's what happened to it. Maybe it got lost. But who loses their
Christmas tree stand? Who is that irresponsible? It doesn't really
matter, because either way, it's gone.

"It's not that bad, Mom," Owen says, shutting off the vacuum cleaner and staring at me as if I were about to dissolve. "We're almost done. You don't have to empty the garbage. Really. I'll do it."

Without the blare of the vacuum cleaner his brothers hear me crying and, dust rags in hand, come into the living room to investigate.

"We need a Christmas tree, you guys," I blubber.

"What's so sad about that?" Will asks.

I wipe my face with a paper towel, then blow my nose on it. Owen, bless his nearly grown-up heart, sees that I am a breath away from crying again and answers for me.

"Moms are just like that, okay?" he explains to Will. "They get all emotional over Christmas. Because they . . . love it so much."

Ever since we moved to the Big Valley when Owen and Luke were little, our tradition has been to cut our own Christmas tree fresh from our woods, the biggest one we can find that will still fit through the door, and then we put it up and decorate it together. But most of our tools were Mr. Wonderful's, and I don't think we have a handsaw big enough to do the job anymore. The hatchet is dull again from all the firewood chopping, and besides, even if we sharpened it, it still couldn't make the clean cut required for a tree to fit in the stand. Then again, we don't have a stand anymore, anyway, so what's the point?

I manage to explain all this to the boys, minus the tears. They look at me like they can't believe I am getting so upset about something so minor. Because what I view as defeat, they consider just another problem to be solved. Not only that, but a problem that is actually far more enjoyable to work on than housecleaning.

"We've got a whole woods right there," Owen says, pointing

out the picture window toward our little woodlot. "I'm sure we've got *something* that can cut down a tree."

"Yeah, like karate chopping!" Will suggests, offering an immediate example with his hands of how this could work. With sound effects.

"Would you get real?" Owen says, though, like me, he can't help laughing.

Luke says nothing, but I can tell he's thinking. Math and the space-time continuum might stymie him, but he's all over practical problems like this one.

I should have known that all I had to do was share this challenge with my sons, because leave it to them to come up with a solution. And once again I am reminded of that basic lesson: the one that says knowing how bad things are is better than not knowing.

Except this time, in our clean house, on a snowy December afternoon, with Christmas bearing down on us, there's a second lesson, too. Knowing how bad things are, and sharing that knowledge with my sons, is a lot better than shouldering it all alone.

"Okay," Luke says, "I got it. What we need is a really big bucket and some rocks."

Luke's idea sends us first to the shop and then to the woods; and the boys, the dogs, and I bivouac through squeaky new snow to the far corner of our woodlot and pick out a tree. It's huge. A white pine, tall and stout, with lacy blue-green needles and thick branches covered with pinecones.

White pines produce a lot of sap, enough to gum up most tree stands, and their branches are too flexible to hold big ornaments or heavy lights, so they aren't very popular as commercial

Christmas trees. They are Michigan's official state tree, though, and their delicate needles are the softest of any evergreen. That sap won't matter to us because of what Luke has rigged up for a stand, and we don't have many heavy ornaments anymore, anyway, so a white pine it is.

The boys and I take turns hacking around the trunk with the dull hatchet, then Owen and Luke grip a branch halfway up on either side, bend the whole tree down this way and that until it finally breaks off near the frozen ground. The end of the trunk is all jagged and the bark is torn, but I already know that won't even matter.

It gets dark so early now, and the light is fading over the hill as we drag our prize back to the house with Will and the dogs in the lead.

"I call putting on the star," Will says as we pull the fat pine through the front door, dumping snow and dirt and pinecones all over our clean floor.

In a snap it's ready for its corner, where Luke has already set up our makeshift stand: a white, five-gallon bucket of joint compound he found in the shop, set up in the corner, and filled with fist-sized rocks we chipped out of the frozen ground.

Will holds the bucket steady while his brothers and I grunt, lift the tree up, and jam its ragged trunk as straight down as we can into the rocks, then anxiously let go. We hold our breath and watch as the tree stands there steady for a moment, then slowly leans away from the staircase and out toward the center of the room, and mercifully stops before it tips over. The leaning tower of Christmas.

Before any of us have time to think, Luke runs up to his bedroom and returns a second later with a handful of thick rope.

What thirteen-year-old boy keeps a length of perfectly coiled purple climbing rope in his bedroom? I shake my head in wonder that my son does.

He lassos a top branch and pulls the loop tight while we straighten the tree, and then he ties off the other end of his rope to a staircase bannister. It holds, the tree is straight, and we can't help cheering.

"Yeah, baby!" Owen says, standing back to admire our work. Luke has gone to the sink with a juice pitcher for water to fill our bucket tree stand, and Will is digging through the ornament box in search of the star for the top.

Our tradition is intact, mostly. But no one is going to mistake this scene for something out of a magazine. The tree is so big, it takes up most of the room. The unfinished staircase reveals raw wood and torn plaster in the background. The purple climbing rope isn't going anywhere and looks out of place next to all the red and green. Plus, we've put up our tree weeks later than we usually do.

And yet, in spite of all this, as far as I'm concerned, it's still the very best Christmas tree we've ever had. It might be the very best Christmas tree *anybody* has ever had.

I have an early-December birthday, and so part of our tradition was to cut the tree and put it up on that day. My birthday was three weeks ago, though, and so it's way too late for that part of our holiday tradition—an oversight that doesn't bother the boys any, if they even remember it, but is something, even with everything else we're struggling with, that I actually miss. For solace, I concoct a makeshift remedy.

While the boys decorate our tree with our only set of lights, several strings of popcorn we've just made, old ribbons from my sewing box, and a few ornaments, I turn on the CD player. A little jolly music in the background, while Owen lifts Will to place the star, will make this holiday scene complete.

There are two popular singers who share a birthday with me. Not the year, but the month and the day. Andy Williams and Ozzy Osbourne. Personality-wise, this fits. I've always thought that I fall about exactly in the middle of these two singers, and I load a CD by each man into the CD player, press the Shuffle button, then Play, so the machine will alternate back and forth between them.

It's the most wonderful time of the year, and I'm going off the rails on a crazy train. But that's nothing to cry over, right? Not at Christmastime. And not here in front of our mighty tree.

The boys and I spend Christmas Day together, just the four of us. In the years to come their father and I will cooperate and alternate holidays, but this year Christmas belongs to me. It belongs to the four of us. The boys spend the daylight hours putting the presents they made at school for me and for each other under our big pine tree, watching Christmas specials on TV, shoveling the walkways, making snowmen, and decorating holiday cookies while I finish cleaning. Late in the afternoon, as it is getting dark, I tell them to suit up, we're having Christmas dinner outside this year.

"We'll need some firewood," I tell the two older boys. "Grab a flashlight and meet us down in the valley."

For some reason I imagine the reaction such an announcement would invite in children not my own, and the images of generic but shocked-faced boys make me smile. My own sons aren't even fazed. They are game for this excursion, even on Christmas. Even with the light fading and the temperature dropping they are game. Their official last name is not Link, they have their father's last name, but in their hearts they are another generation of Links.

"Keep your dobbers up!" was the last thing my dad said to me before the boys and I pulled out of my parents' driveway, loaded down with all those presents.

This is what my dad has always said to me whenever I've needed encouragement, from the time I was a little girl. When I got a bad grade on a test or dropped a fly ball or got dumped by my boyfriend. I don't know what a dobber is exactly, but I do know that my sons are keeping theirs up. They get the job done right. They don't complain.

Owen holds the flashlight for his brother while Luke collects another armful of kindling. Bundled in their snow pants and their puffy jackets, hoods up, making their way over an incandescent landscape with the black horizon behind, they look like teen astronauts collecting specimens on the moon.

Tonight I am going to teach Will how to build a one-match fire. He and I head down to the bottom of the valley, where there's no wind. We can hear his brothers crunching a path toward us through the high drifts. The woodpile is stacked next to our garage at the top of the hill, but our fire pit is down in a little clearing in our valley, surrounded by pine trees, dormant grass asleep under the heavy snow, and silence.

Owen and Luke already know how to build a one-match fire, and I've sent them for the firewood so that Will can build his very first one without any "help" or observations from his older brothers. Loaded up with the wood, they are on their way back down.

A crust has formed on top of the snow, and it is strong enough to support their teen bodies for only a moment, but then it gives way and their legs plunge down with a crunch and they are up to their knees again, first one leg, then the other.

The beam of their flashlight bounces off the snow, rockets through the trees, and shines down toward earth, and us. The light syncopates in time with their laughing.

"Get going, Little Red Riding Dork," teases Owen, his laughter echoing.

"Oh, that is *snow* funny," Luke says, and I can hear the smile in his voice.

Just for tonight I wish I could forget that they are covering the same ground that the real-estate appraiser did, but I can't quite manage it.

It snowed the day he was here. I know this because he left his footprints behind. After we arrived home from celebrating Christmas with my parents, the appraiser came back for a second visit, and I watched out the window while he walked all around the property in a flapping black coat and wing-tip shoes. The wind blew his hat off, blew the papers off his clipboard, blew the stringy wisps of his black hair off his bare scalp and straight up into the air.

His first visit was December 21, the winter solstice, the shortest, darkest day of the year. Probably just a coincidence, I told myself, while I stood in front of our big picture window the next evening and watched him slip and fall on our iced-over driveway. Owen saw him, too, but neither one of us went outside to help the man.

"Count Olaf is in our yard," Owen said, referencing the villain from the story I'd been reading aloud in the evenings to his two younger brothers. It makes me smile to think of him, a teenager with a rock band, long hair, and driver's ed, listening in from his bedroom.

Night and snowfall and the booted feet of my firewood-carrying children have erased Count Olaf's tracks completely, but I know that they are still there, smoldering like dry ice somewhere deep. While most people probably want their houses to be worth a lot of money, I do not. The more the Big Valley is worth, the more Mr. Wonderful's half is also worth, and the less chance I have of being qualified for a mortgage on it.

"You only have one chance, so you have to get everything just right before you light the match," I tell Will.

"Mom, you've got a whole box," he says, looking at the cardboard container of stick matches in my hand.

"I have a whole box *right now*," I tell him. "But you never know when you might be down to your very last one."

A one-match fire is just that: a fire built using only a single match and what nature provides. No crumpled-up newspaper, no treated logs, no fire-starting sticks, no lighters, no gasoline from the lawn mower or lighter fluid. No second tries.

Fires can be started without any matches at all, of course, with just friction and patience, but I've always figured that if you don't have a single match and you're stuck outside in the winter in Michigan, you're pretty much done for, friction or no friction.

Will accepts the seriousness of his task big-eyed and silent, bends down and makes a mound with his gloved hands out of the dead pine needles we've collected. His snowsuit rustles as I show him how to pile the needles on top of a raft of dry branches so that when the needles burn and heat up the frozen ground underneath, the melting snow won't extinguish the fire before it even has a chance to get going.

"Okay, now make the triangle like I showed you, overtop."

His brothers appear out of the dark and Luke drops his armful of logs and kindling while Owen stows the flashlight in his pocket. Stick by skinny stick Will builds the fire while we watch, until a symmetrical little pyramid of dry wood stands a foot and a half tall in the center of this area we've cleared in the snow.

I reach in my pocket and pull out the single stick match and hand it to Will. He takes off his glove and gives it a solid scratch against the zipper of his coat. It lights and he touches it to the edge of his mound of pine needles, blows on them, and they catch fire, smoking, crackling, and curling a glowing red.

"Mom! It's working!" he says, and I don't think he could be any more amazed if he had pointed a magic wand at the pile of sticks and they ignited. The pine needles catch the tiny twigs, the twigs catch the larger sticks around the pyramid, and then the whole pyramid begins to flame. Instinctively, the four of us are already standing in a circle, looking into the center, and soon heat and light spread to our fronts. The dark can have our backs, and does.

I remember the bonfire I lit months ago in our front yard. All it did was kill the grass and leave a big scorch mark. At least the boys didn't witness that one. This fire is something else, though, something unifying. This fire, small and under control, has a practical use and is more than just a lesson in match management and winter survival.

My frayed red daypack hangs on a nearby tree branch. In it is our Christmas dinner: a package of Rocky hot dogs (my sons have forbidden me from ever calling them "wieners"), a Tofurky dog for Owen, a package of hot dog buns, ketchup, mustard, four small apples, all the ingredients for S'mores, and four metal roasting forks.

We take turns adding bigger and bigger logs, until the fire burns so hot that we take off our jackets. Sparks float upward. Our woods, so loud with birdsong and squirrel chatter and road noise during the day, is absolutely silent tonight. The snow dripping off the trees like meringue muffles everything, even the sound of the fire and of our own breathing. We're protected in this valley, this big valley, the namesake of our little farm, at least for tonight.

I launch into a round of "Silent Night," and the boys join in, but not for long. When we get to the part about the "round yon Virgin," Owen starts snickering, Luke follows suit and Will asks what a virgin is anyway and what's so funny, the infant with holes in it?, and the song falls apart. It must be time to eat.

We made it through this year, I silently pray, *barely—please let us make it through the next one, too.*

Around the circle are stumps cut flat long ago by someone else with a chain saw, and they are good stools. I make a show of pulling out our red-and-green, gold-flecked holiday tablecloth with a flourish, fold it in thirds, and drape it over the biggest stump. Our holiday table.

As soon as there are coals I unpack our supplies and dole them out. Everyone gets a hot dog to roast, and I line up the buns on the stump table and set out the ketchup, mustard, and apples.

"We're like the hoboes," Owen says, sliding his soy dog onto his roasting fork and holding it over the fire. "Just free and out on the land."

Will leans back on his stump and looks up at the night sky. I look where he is looking and so does Luke and we see the Milky

Way. The Big Valley is far enough away from the lights of town that this celestial pathway is often visible on cloudless nights like this one, especially in the winter.

It isn't late, only dinnertime, probably seven or seven-thirty, but it has already been dark for what seems like hours. The heat has made pink circles on Will's cheeks, he's taken off his hat, and his blond hair is sticking out from the static. It isn't the North Star or any particular constellation or a satellite that he sees when he looks up, but an entirely different kind of celestial being.

"Santa's up there right now," he says, his voice filled with the magic of this instant, of Christmas, and of the fire he built himself but that is feeding all of us. Anything should be possible on such a night, shouldn't it? Even having your youngest son, who will turn nine years old in less than a week, still believe in Santa Claus.

I hold my breath and wait for his brothers to laugh at him, or say something sarcastic, or in some other way break the spell, but there is only the crackling sound of the fire, and the colored lights decorating our porch up on the hill, and the faraway stars like sequins sprinkled on this purple velvet sky floating a million miles above our heads.

I've hung the boys' Christmas stockings on the fireplace mantel, but they are pretty empty. Gift cards I got for free from my bank by cashing in the points I've earned all year by paying for gas and groceries with my debit card, some candy, and a few music CDs I burned from my computer.

"What's a hobo again?" Luke asks. He's eating his Rocky hot dog with his gloves on, and there is ketchup smeared on his nylon fingers.

"You know, guys who are poor, but they don't know they're poor," Owen says. "They don't have cars or houses or jobs or anything, so they go around having adventures and camping out and stuff."

I look through the trees and up the hill toward our house. It seems so far away, but I know it's right there. I've left the porch light on. Inside, the house smells wintery-good, like the pine cleaner from my mother and the pine needles from our fresh-cut tree.

A few feet from the Christmas stockings, on top of a stack of bills on the sewing-machine table I use for a desk, is a legal-sized envelope addressed to me. The seal has been broken and there is a ten-page document inside. It looks harmless enough, but for all the destruction it contains, it might as well be a mail bomb.

It's the official appraisal of our farm, and it arrived yesterday afternoon, Christmas Eve. According to the balding appraiser with the snow-ruined wing-tip shoes, our farmhouse, outbuildings, and land are worth $312,800.

"Mom, is that really what a hobo is?" Luke asks.

Nope, I think, there's actually a little more to it than that. Because you can be a mother who lives in a house that's apparently worth a small fortune, but if you still can't offer your sons any-thing better than hot dogs for Christmas dinner, that can qualify you as a kind of hobo, too. Or at least make you feel like one.

But of course I can't say this to Luke.

"Yeah," I tell him instead. "Pretty much."

7

January 2006

WOLF MOON

Love will find a way through paths where wolves fear to prey.

—LORD BYRON

Two weeks after Christmas, it begins. It's late on a Monday morning and it starts with an ache buried real deep, somewhere along the axis that runs down my neck and in between my shoulder blades. In hours every muscle in my body feels worked over by the wrong end of a claw hammer. By the time Owen and Luke get home from school, just before four o'clock, I'm upstairs in my bedroom, in bed, fully clothed, shivering and sweating, under a wool comforter. I've slept most of the day and I'm still exhausted.

The mortgage is two months overdue, but work is going to be missed, deadlines are going to be missed, assignments not turned in, invoices not sent.

"Watch TV," I mumble to the kids from somewhere deep in my pillow. This command is a bigger clue to them that something is amiss than the sight of me in bed in the middle of the day. They've seen me take a late-afternoon nap before, although not too often, but a directive that they turn on the idiot box in the afternoon on a school day? A Monday no less, just a couple of weeks after their holiday break with homework assignments galore? Pure craziness.

The boys are not allowed to watch television or play video games during the week. When they were babies, they didn't sit in front of any screens, at all, ever, not a one of them. We owned one television set, but it was stored on the floor in the closet. Reception never has been too good in there, which was exactly the point.

I wanted my sons to do what I did as a kid—read books, climb trees, build forts, play kick-the-can, and skin their knees sliding into second—not spend their childhoods in front of a screen.

Our TV was eventually dusted off and brought out into the open for one reason and one reason only: so that I could watch football. (If I'm ever given one of those questionnaires that ask me to reveal something about myself that few people know, I'd put down "rabid Detroit Lions fan." Someday we will be in the Super Bowl. And win.)

After football season, the idiot box stayed out of the closet and was eventually hooked up to basic cable. Owen and Luke were in elementary school by then, and Will was in preschool, but the boys were allowed to watch only a limited amount of television (an hour per day), and even then only on the weekends.

So of course they are stunned when today I'm actually *telling* them to turn the thing on. Usually when they get home from school I'm prompting them toward, first, a snack, then their homework, then music practice, then their chores, then, if there's time, going out to play. If it's bad weather, they can read a book, play a board game, bake with me, or do a craft project.

In their defense, when I tell them to go watch TV, they do seem a little worried about me; yet they still can't believe their luck and waste no time thundering down the stairs, running into the family room, and body-slamming each other for the remote. Will won't be home for another hour, so it's just the two of them. I don't actually see any of this activity, I only hear it, because I can't move from the warm magnet that is my bed.

So what, I rationalize, as my eyelids begin to latch themselves shut again. So they'll watch some *Dragon Ball Z* or *Captain Planet* for a couple of hours. Just this one time. How bad can that really be? I know they've watched these programs at their friends' houses, and they don't seem any worse for wear afterward.

But just as I'm about to fold back into my influenza coma, the sound of deviant stoner cartoon laughter filters upstairs and into my fading consciousness, now located in some distant land between my twin earaches. Through the mung I hear two TV voices chortle and then have an exchange along these lines:

"Uh, I have an injury. Huh-huh-huh."

"You do? Heh-heh."

"Yeah, I have this great big crack in my butt. Eh-heh-heh."

My two older sons are fifteen and thirteen now. And their virgin ears have just been breached by MTV's couch-sitting anti-heroes, Beavis and Butt-head. Or, if you prefer, "Ass-munch" and "Bung-hole." Help me, Jesus.

I don't have the energy to halt this or even comment on it, and after I register what they're watching, I fall back asleep. Was this objectionable program still on the TV when Will, who turned nine right after Christmas, came home an hour later? Who knows.

Did I fix them any dinner? Probably not, and the next several days pass with me in feverish suspension, not awake but not asleep, either. What do they eat? How do they get ready for school? Who helps them with their homework? I don't know.

I have one memory of standing at the front window in sweatpants, watching Will stand at the bus stop, in the dark, in a snowstorm, alone. I see the bus slow to a stop, the light go on inside the bus as the hinged door opens, I see Will's backlit form walking up the steps out of the swirling snow and into safety, and then I collapse on the couch for the rest of that day and maybe for the next one, too.

I know Will doesn't miss a single hour of school the whole ten days I am sick, because he receives an award for being one of only two kids in his entire elementary school of more than three hundred students with perfect attendance. How did he manage this? How did his brothers? I don't know.

By luck, the flu strikes when their father and I have switched weekends, and so the boys are here with me for two weeks straight. They bring glasses of water and juice upstairs and stand watch while I drink them. Owen makes me a cheese sandwich, which I can't even think of eating, and Will brings me a sweaty handful of Fritos. He knows they are my favorite. In another life I could eat half a bag. I eat two, maybe three chips.

CNN must be on, because I hear recurring headlines that nauseate me further: if we are headed for a recession, Michigan will feel it earlier, deeper, and longer than the rest of the country; Ford is closing fourteen auto plants and cutting a quarter of its Michigan workforce; and mad cow disease is spreading through Canada, perhaps heading our way.

Is there such a thing as mad pig disease? I consider the last shankburger from Rocky that I ate—was it too rare?—before I fall asleep again.

The flu bug keeps right on biting me through the weekend, unabated. I am too sick to even wonder what I've been infected with after that contaminated-meat headline fades. Later I will learn that I don't have food poisoning, I have a virus. And I will eventually understand that virus's probable ancestry when its spread becomes the medical story of the moment.

In September a teenage boy butchered pigs at a slaughterhouse in Sheboygan, Wisconsin, some ninety miles southwest and across Lake Michigan from my sweaty bedroom. I can see a bay of this very body of water out the window from the sickbed I've taken to. The Wisconsin pig slaughterer is stricken with a bad flu virus, later found to be unlike any ever before encountered by medical science—a mutation of the swine flu—and I'm pretty sure this microscopic freeloader migrated—yes, maybe even flew—its evil piggy self across the water and into what feels like every single one of my cells.

How is it that a bout with the flu can take me down so completely?

I can do pain. I'm actually the stuff of extended family legend where pain tolerance is concerned. After Will was born via emergency C-section, a nurse on duty in the maternity ward overlooked that teensy-weensy detail called an IV drip. For the first eight hours after surgery, my nervous system was flying commando. No fluids, no anti-inflammatories, no pain meds at all, not even a baby aspirin. It wasn't until the nurse on duty *the day after* my surgery noticed that I didn't have an IV and opened a drawer in the cabinet next to my bed and found my unused bag of new-mommy drugs inside that I knew something was amiss.

I just had my core sliced open from hip to hip, pain was to be expected, right? I just ground my teeth and bore it. I didn't complain, I kept my dobbers up. But this flu is even worse than that and it is taking me down.

The boys keep me in fluids and Tylenol, bless their beating hearts, and somehow keep themselves fed, dressed, and in school. One night Will comes upstairs and reads me a chapter of the book I was reading to him before I got sick. The lost china rabbit is now in the care of a girl with a mean father and a bad cough.

Another night Luke stands at the foot of my bed and models the costume he made for history day at school. He is going as Albert Einstein, of course. He uses a fuzzy gray hat of mine for the hair and is wearing a white button-down shirt and the black dress pants he grew out of last year that I was saving to hand down to Will. I point at his naked ankles sticking out of his leather dress shoes. Apparently, even in January, one does not need socks to understand the structure of the universe. Einstein didn't believe in time and it looks like he didn't believe in socks, either.

"That's why I chose him," Luke says. "I don't have any clean ones."

I still have plenty of the laundry detergent from the box of domestic supplies my mother gave me for Christmas. Just no strength to do any laundry.

The boys ask no one for help. The Link motto of accountability, of dobbers up, head down, soldier on, has obviously been passed down to them. By late Monday, a full week into my flu, the three of them can't keep us going alone any longer, and Owen wakes me up in the middle of the night.

"Mom," he says, pressing his hand on my arm. I feel his presence, but am slow on the uptake. "Mom!" he says again, shaking me now.

I wake up thinking, *Is something on fire? Did the horses get out? Burglar?*

These are just sleep-drugged worries that have no truck with reality. There is no fire; there are no horses, not anymore; and burglar—are you kidding me? What do we have to steal? Not a darn thing. Rifling through these thoughts, I finally make sleepy eye contact with my oldest.

"We're out of food," he says.

I can't figure out why Owen wants to eat in the middle of the night. I look at the clock. It's not the middle of the night after all, it's only 8:30 in the evening. It just feels like the middle of the night because it's dark outside and I've lost all sense of time. My arms and legs feel like lake-sunk trees, my head a stuffy, water-logged bowling ball sunk in sheets awash in my own chilly sweat.

At least the fever broke. The smell makes me think that maybe I can do laundry, after all.

"We're out of milk, we don't have any cereal or cheese or apples or anything," he tells me.

"Nothing?" I mumble through chapped lips.

He shakes his head.

"When did you guys eat?"

"At school, and then when we got home we had macaroni and cheese. I microwaved it."

"Hungry?" I ask. He nods.

Owen sits down on the edge of the bed and waits while I gather my resolve, which takes a long time considering there's not too much of it to round up.

"I can drive if you guys can shop," I tell him.

Help, I think. *I need some help.*

But I make it to the driver's seat of our van with my winter coat and boots slipped on over my sour-smelling pajamas. The fever is definitely gone, so are the earaches and the sore throat, I'm just weak. In my coat pocket is our last sixty-five dollars. I won't get paid for another ten days and not at all if I don't start churning out some work. That sixty-five dollars has to last us until then.

I don't want to waste any energy making a list, so on the drive to the grocery store I tell my sons what to buy and Owen writes it down.

A gallon of 2 percent milk.

Two boxes of cereal, their choice.

Fruit, yogurt, juice.

A can of lentil soup, I think I could eat that.

Peanut butter, cheese, eggs, tortillas, hummus.

Maybe some more Fritos, if there's enough money.

Owen is sitting in the passenger seat, and I put the money in his hand. "Don't go over, because this is all we've got," I tell him weakly. He nods.

He can't come back to the van to get more money, because we don't have any more. I can't just write a check if he goes over, because it will bounce. I can't transfer money from savings to checking, because there is no savings.

I park right in front of the store, driving over the words "No Parking—Fire Lane," and turn off the ignition to save gas. Just driving here has exhausted me, and I hope I'll have enough energy to get us home. Owen doesn't have his license yet and isn't supposed to drive with just his temporary permit after dark.

"I'll be right here," I say to Owen, then turn to Luke and Will in the backseat. "Boys, listen to your brother. He's in charge.

No arguing in the store, no goofing around. Say thank you to the cashier. Don't forget."

"It'll be good, Mom," Owen reassures me as they all three solemnly exit the van. "It'll be fine."

The grocery store has large glass windows all along the front, and I watch as Owen gets a shopping cart and his brothers take their posts, one at each of his shoulders.

They've shopped with me many times before, all three of them, and I've sent the two older boys into the corner store together to pick up one or two items while I wait in the minivan, but I've never asked them to do this. I've never asked them to shop like adults—to go through the whole store with a cart and a set amount of money and select several days' worth of groceries all alone, and then to pay for them and carry them out of the store and load them in the van by themselves.

I know that my SMILE handbook lists the top five ways that parents can help their children adjust to divorce, because I've practically memorized them by now. This is number one: "A parent should not depend on their children for emotional support. Children need to be children."

I *so* want to be that mother, the one SMILE holds out as the ideal. Yet often, like now, I find myself doing the exact opposite of her, and I know it.

Over the next half hour the car grows cold and I ache and shiver as I catch glimpses of my trio inside the store, making their way from aisle to aisle. Children may need to be children, but in these brief sightings, they don't look like children to me anymore, they look like small, skinny adults. Something in the way they hold themselves. The way they walk straight ahead, no wiggling, no wasted motion.

I've been sick for eight days, and at some point during each one of those I asked for help, but I've asked for it mostly silently, so no one can hear me. Twice, though, I've asked for it out loud.

I called a friend and told her I was sick and probably dehydrated and she drove over and left a two-liter of 7Up on my front porch but didn't come inside—she has small children of her own, one just two years old, and didn't want them to get sick, too.

I called a doctor, but it was on the weekend, he was an on-call physician and not my regular doctor, and he chastised me a good one for waiting too long to ask for help. He was sure I had a new and particularly severe strain of flu, but it was too late for him to do anything for me. If I'd called sooner, then maybe he could have helped. "Now," he tells me, in a sovereign tone, "you're just going to have to suffer through."

Tell me something I don't know, Ass-munch.

There is no one else. My friend Beverly is gone on a mission trip to Africa, so I can't call her to come help us. Another friend, Linda, is working 24/7, plus she doesn't drive in the winter anymore, after a harrowing near miss with a snowplow. My parents live 150 miles away. My brother and his new girlfriend are who knows where, doing who knows what. I don't have many neighbors, and the few I do have I either don't know or don't like.

And then, this final realization hits me hard: for all my spiritual searching over the past several months through a mysterious Eastern religion, looking for some fuzzy thing I've been thinking of as my divine nature, we don't even have a regular old midwestern Protestant church with a real building and real people to go to and ask for real help.

It occurs to me too, watching my boys push the half-full shopping cart up to the cashier's lane and load each item onto the conveyor belt, that they're not much for asking for help, either. Not a one of them. This, I know from my own stubborn self, will yield both rewards and consequences in their grown-up lives. And there's probably nothing I can do to spare them the latter. No one could have spared me.

The grocery store's automatic air lock door swooshes open, I turn the minivan's engine back on, and out come my sons, my heroes, small, medium, and large, loaded down with bags of provisions. In an evenly spaced line all three totter under their burdens single-file, past the front of the minivan, jogging through my headlight beams.

I have this piece of a memory then. Once a long time ago, before kids, before a husband, I drove into the parking lot of an apartment complex at night, my headlights sweeping over parked cars, snowed-over front steps, and lighted windows with the drapes closed. I don't even remember where it was or why I was there. Out from between two of the buildings came three adolescent raccoons tiptoeing through the night, treats in their humanoid front paws no doubt pilfered from a nearby Dumpster. Snowdrifts shone, tiny stars lit the night, and the very air glittered in the cold. For a few quiet minutes no one but those raccoons and I were in the world.

I put the car in park and watched as the young furry bandits walked a few steps past my headlights single-file, little bodies up on their hind legs, black hands clutching the food to their chests. From around the corner of the building came the mother raccoon, sniffing the air and greeting each cub nose-to-nose. The four of them ate together right there in the cold starlight, then she took her place at the front of the line and led her brood off into some scraggly nearby woods and they disappeared from my sight.

Just a family, heading home, through the frozen dark.

I unlock the doors of the van and the boys climb inside, pulling their shopping bags in with them. Owen hands me a few dollar bills and some coins, then turns to face the backseat.

"Tell her," he says to his brothers.

No response.

"Tell her!" Owen says again.

"We got cookies," Luke confesses.

"Two bags," Will adds. "Oreos."

"I told them they weren't on the list," Owen says to me, apologetic.

The car goes silent, waiting for my reaction. We don't buy store-bought cookies. If the boys want cookies, they have to do the work of making them from scratch. Peanut butter chocolate chip usually, with fork marks across the top, like paw prints.

"Cookies are cool," I say in my very best Beavis voice. The boys all laugh. A laugh of silliness, but a laugh of relief, too. "Please hand me one, somebody, before I die of starvation."

"Heh-heh—heh-heh-heh," comes the trio's reply.

They are all the help I need. And I feel a little bit better just thinking this thought. We pass no one on the drive back, and eat sugary store-bought cookies in the cold dark together as our minivan shoots home like a glittering missile.

We are okay, we are fine. I am fine. Mothers are mothers again and children are children. And it feels like there's no one but the four of us in the world.

8

February 2006

HUNGER MOON

Awake at last, the body begins to crave,
not salads, not crisp apples and sweet kiwis,
but haunches of beef and thick fatty stews.
Eat, whispers the crone in the bone, eat.
The hunger moon is grinning like a skull.

—MARGE PIERCY, "The Hunger Moon"

The groceries don't last. The carrots packed in sawdust don't last. Our firewood doesn't last. Our money certainly doesn't last, either. As if I needed any further proof that we are scraping bottom, I'm making Will's sack lunch for school and have to mine the sides of the peanut butter jar just to get enough of the stuff to make him half a sandwich.

I hold up the spoon and stare at this glob of caramel-colored paste, looking for a sign. A week ago, our newspaper ran an interview with an Ohio man who said he saw the face of Jesus in his pancake. I don't see anything in our last spoonful of extra-crunchy, though.

Even if there were something (or Someone) there, would my cynical brain even allow my heart to see it?

The boys didn't get sick but I'm still reeling a little from the flu. Still, we went to a tiny church last Sunday just down the road. Will read the sign on the door and announced this sudden realization: a god and a prince are one and the same. I smiled, thinking how meaningful it was going to be to pray alongside people from our own neighborhood and in the denomination—Lutheran— that I was raised within.

But instead of a friendly welcome, the Prince of Peace just barred me from taking communion, and right after an usher passed around the collection plate, too. Unless visitors would pledge membership on the spot, no wine and no wafer. This place didn't feel like our church home after all, it felt more like the rural branch of a stodgy old bank. And our souls just got bounced.

"But Mom, that was just a *piece* of the Prince," Will suggests, wincing at my loud tirade over religious dogma that I miraculously managed to stifle until the car ride home. "Now we just need to find the rest of him."

At least one of us might be learning something valuable— forgiveness—on our continuing spiritual quest. I guess it shouldn't matter if it's not always me.

That plain old peanut butter jar probably divines our fortunes better than church rules or a hokey spiritual sign, anyway. And there is a reason the jar was empty. My grocery bill just went back up, because last week we suffered a loss.

"What's that smell?" Owen had asked, the first one home from school.

"What smell?" My head was still congested, and so I didn't smell anything.

"Like rotten flowers or something. I think it's coming from the basement."

It was.

While I was sick with that awful flu, the Big Valley lost power when a thick bludgeon of ice built up on a nearby power line. The electricity was out for only a few hours, not even long enough for what little food we had in our refrigerator to go bad, but long enough for our ancient chest freezer in the basement to die. When the power went back on, it didn't.

In the past two weeks I've been getting stronger and getting my appetite back, but meat is the last thing I've wanted to eat, and it's been vegetables and brown rice, farmer's omelets and peanut butter toast. I can't eat any pork yet, I can't even stomach cooking it for the boys, so I've had no reason to go downstairs and lift the lid on the chest freezer.

Until now. Until the smell.

Owen and I approach the white coffin-shaped box with dread, open the top, and are blown back by the sweet, gagging stink of rotting pork. We look down, but it's too late. A pinkish meat Kool-Aid has leaked out under the freezer and pooled. We're standing in it.

"Okay, that's about the grossest thing I've ever seen," Owen says, holding his hand over his face and race-walking for the stairs. This from the politically aware vegetarian who has watched the most graphic animal-rights videos available on the Internet and has somehow still remained emotionally sound. The smell of rancid pig juice is too much for him, though, and he exits quick.

I am not a crier. I will not cry. I didn't cry over our cold house, I didn't cry when I had the flu, and I didn't even cry when Rocky was offed. I haven't cried since Christmas Eve when I thought we weren't going to have a tree, and I will not cry over spilled meat, either.

What I feel isn't sadness, anyway, but shame—the shame of all that waste.

Some of the meat from our pig we already ate, but the rest was supposed to last us all winter, and now it's spoiled. I can't vouch for the other supplies that were sharing the freezer with him, either. Not the meat I've bought on sale at the grocery store, not some of the frozen vegetables from our garden, not the big slab of venison from my brother's deer-hunting prowess. That's all bad now, too.

What are we going to do for food? I don't know. How many times in one year can a mother say "I will think of something" and actually pull that off all by herself? I guess we are going to find out.

There is still the side-by-side refrigerator/freezer in the kitchen, and the freezer half is packed with the rest of the vegetables from the garden. There is still credit left on the bakery card, and what I've canned and stored in the root cellar. But there aren't going to be any more ham dinners. There's not going to be any more bacon or pork chops.

I think of Rocky in his pen, and it feels like his death was for nothing now.

We still have half our zucchini winnings, so at least we have plenty of bread. But with all our meat gone I have to spend more at the grocery store again. On peanut butter, but on a lot of other sources of protein too, and I am drawn to the two-for-ones, the day-old, the nearly expired, and to that lonely shopping cart of discontinued and dented cans my local grocery store seems to park, for some sadistic reason, in the same aisle as the four-dollar imported spring water from Fiji. Who actually buys that stuff? I almost want to stake out the aisle to find out.

Instead, I paw through the discount cart weekly like a badger at a rotted log. What can you make with two dented cans of sock-eye salmon? Believe me, you'll think of something when they're only twenty-nine cents each.

The boys learn to approach our dinner table with trepidation, not knowing if they'll be greeted with chipped beef on toast, salmon puffs (a recipe handed down from my grandma Hain, who had her own penny-saving culinary strategies), fried tofu, or oyster soup. So far, I haven't tried to make Emergency Steak, but the oyster soup, made from a recipe I find in the newspaper, is just as bad.

I prepare it according to the instructions and ladle the thin gruel into bowls for dinner, but we all just look at it, transfixed, as if peering at an aquarium exhibit gone wrong. What we see is a half-dozen sickly gray bivalves that seem shocked to find themselves stripped of their shells and floating in a milky sea contaminated at the surface with a buttery yellow scum.

"Are those baby clams from Big Grandpa's lake?" Luke wonders out loud.

Eventually, the whole pot is upended over the compost pile. I sit in my chair and watch out the window. Seagulls, and not crows, are sighted that evening, perched atop the volcano-shaped pile, pecking away at the oyster-stew lava. I call Owen over to the window to watch them with me.

"They really will eat anything, won't they?" he says, amazed.

With our dwindling rations, we probably should have eaten it. Instead, we have microwave popcorn, apples, and of course peanut butter. For dinner. On a Sunday.

I think of the Sunday dinners my mother and my grandmothers used to cook when I was my sons' ages. Pot roast, baked ham with scalloped potatoes, chicken pot pie, fried bluegills and homemade coleslaw, barbequed chicken. On my kitchen counter is a recipe box with all these family recipes inside and more. My mother's seafood casserole and her Impossible Brunch Pie, my grandma Link's fried chicken, my grandma Hain's bluegill recipe. I have the kitchen skill to make any of these boy-satiating dishes, just not the money. That broken freezer is going to haunt us for months.

Lunches for the week are going to be problematic too, I can tell, both by the empty peanut butter jar and by the wide-open spaces in the cupboards. Behind their closed doors, it's like an open range in there. Checking my work with *Finding Utopia*, and from the freelance writing assignments I've turned in recently, I know that I will not bring in a paycheck for two weeks.

So that's it, then. It has to be done.

The next morning after Owen and Luke get on the bus for school, I sweep fresh snow off my van with a broom and drive Will to his elementary school. Instead of just dropping him off at the front door I park and walk him inside. We separate in the lobby and he heads to his third-grade classroom with a tossed-off "See ya" (I am recently forbidden to hug him in public) and I head to the school office.

On my list of favorite people, the school secretary falls somewhere south of Nurse Ratched. I have it on good authority that she frightens the new principal. Get a nosebleed, a tardy, or forget your gym shoes and prepare for isolation therapy.

Every single time I've been in the school office there's been a kid sitting in an orange plastic chair in a small room five feet from the school secretary's desk, crying softly, or holding a bloody tissue to his or her nose, or both. No one is allowed to speak to or look at this kid. At least, that's the vibe communicated to lowly moms like me by Nurse Ratched's raised and frosted eyebrow.

And this is the woman I have come before today in an attempt to ease my grocery budget shortfall. After standing at the counter that separates her desk from the outside world for what feels like the time it takes to make a transcontinental flight I almost bloody my own nose and go sit in the orange chair—strangely vacant—myself before she finally acknowledges me.

"Yessss?"

Several years from now she will get divorced and morph into a decent person in a transformation as complete as the one the Incredible Hulk undergoes when he loses his green-veined muscles and his bad attitude, prompting many moms to nod their heads in understanding, me included. At this moment, though, with the task at hand, that bit of personal growth is unforeseen.

"I'd like an application for the free and reduced lunch program, please," I tell her.

This gets her attention. Am I secretly miked? Because I swear my voice sounds like it was just broadcast over the school PA system. Is the principal's office door really open, and do I really see her peek her head out and back like a seesaw? Are the children in coats and snow pants holding the folded flag they are about to raise outside at the pole really staring? At me? In the sage words of Henry Kissinger, even the paranoid have enemies.

Approval for the free lunches is not, I know, going to be a

problem. Standing here asking for the application is the problem. My pride is the problem.

According to the Friend of the Court, which monitors the well-being of children of divorced parents in Grand Traverse County and points us in the direction of help, I now qualify for Federal Food Assistance Programs, the Child Care and Development Fund, Medicaid, the Home Heating Credit, the Low Income Home Energy Assistance Program, the Weatherization Assistance Program, free venison from Hunters for the Hungry, and even government cheese.

I have applied for none of it. I have told myself that these programs are for other people. For other families. They are for the really poor families, the ones who live in the trailers and campers. The ones who keep their dogs tied on chains and don't brush their kids' hair and have rusty roll bars on their trucks and broken refrigerators on their front porches. Not, in other words, for me. Not for us.

This is the same way I felt about divorce once. It was for other troubled couples, not for Mr. Wonderful and me.

"Excuse me?" the school secretary says, interested now and pushing her long frosted hair behind her ears. So she can hear me better, I surmise, just in case I grovel.

"Reduced—lunch—application," I say, through teeth gritted behind a forced smile.

"Oh, *certainly*." She passes the fluorescent form (a color that matches the bloody-nose chair and seems to scream "failure") across the counter to me. "Is this for *you*? Because it has to be filled out by the person who is applying for the assistance. You can't fill it out for someone else."

I don't answer, but just put my wool gloves back on, take the form, and go. I fill it out at home and make two copies and mail them in to each of the boys' schools, direct to the principals, bypassing (I hope) Nurse Ratched and her ilk. A week later, all three boys are on the typed list of poor kids that I imagine each lunch lady has laminated and highlighted, hanging next to their cash register.

This, I tell myself, is only temporary. Just like all the rest of our money problems—the late fees, the pre-pre-foreclosure notice I pulled out of the mailbox today, the empty refrigerator, and my recurring night terrors. All temporary, just quick-fix patches to get us through until I can figure out a real solution.

If this is supposed to be the universe's way of teaching me nonattachment, it's not working. And if everything in life really is only temporary, why are our money problems starting to feel like such a permanent condition?

Three days after Valentine's Day I wake up early, get my usual 5 a.m. school-day start going, make the coffee, and plan out my day. Good news: as soon as the kids get off to school this morning, I actually have some work to turn in and some receivables to collect, some paychecks to cash. I also have bills to pay, so this money won't take my sons off the cafeteria dole just yet, but it's a start.

The coffee trickles down and I take a long look outside, waiting for my caffeine infusion. It's as dark as a buzzard's eyeball out there, but snowdrifts reflect light from the waning moon, and I can see just enough to make my heart beat hard, like I just took a snowball to the chest.

This bang inside my rib cage is followed by a perfectly timed retort from above: thundersnow.

Of course. On the *one* day I really, really need to be mobile, we're snowed in.

Thundersnow is a meteorological novelty virtually unknown outside of the Great Lakes. In this twist on the traditional thunderstorm there is still plenty of thunder and lightning, but snow falls instead of rain and functions much like the silencer on a gun. A blizzard of heavy flakes packs the unsettled air and concentrates the storm's atmospheric booms into a small area, intensifying them. This one feels like the Big Valley's own personal storm, whipped up by Thor, the devil, or fate, take your pick, just for us.

Yesterday's forecast included a winter storm warning, but forecasts like that are about as common as ice shanties up here, so I didn't pay much attention. Now the radio announcer says that an overnight blizzard is still blowing, dozens of school districts are closed, including Grand Traverse Public, and we've got two feet of new snow on the ground, some that fell, some that the wind just drifted.

Lightning flickers and I catch glimpses of what I know is out there, but dread just the same: our impassable driveway.

I do the figuring in my head. One hundred feet long by ten feet wide by three feet deep if you include the foot of packed snow that was already there when I went to bed last night. Plus work to deliver and a paycheck that's out there just waiting for me in a nice warm office downtown. All that equals three thousand cubic feet of snow the boys and I have to shovel.

Everywhere in northern Michigan this morning there are schoolchildren, snowmobile dealers, ski-resort owners, and plow-truck drivers clicking their heels together for joy. Everywhere, that is, but here.

I used to love winter. I used to take pride in my ability to withstand the cold. I know how to tuck in and layer. I know how to snowshoe, ice-skate, cross-country-ski, and how to carve around moguls on black-diamond ski hills: activities that took hours and hours of winter days to learn.

But that was when I had parents who took my brother and me on ski vacations and kept a warm house for us to return to, or when I lived in a college dorm with central heating and a maintenance crew, or when Mr. Wonderful and I could afford to heat our house and hire a plowing service.

Today, I feel more like Sir Ernest Shackleton than a snow bunny, and I just wonder how I'm going to get off my property. Because the Big Valley might as well be that explorer's doomed ship trapped in pack ice, frozen to this spot, all of us stuck inside and waiting to be crushed.

I think of Shackleton only because Owen is working on a report about him for school and the research is spread out on our kitchen counter. There's even a copy he printed out from the Internet of an advertisement Shackleton placed nearly a century ago in London newspapers:

MEN WANTED: For hazardous journey.
Small wages, bitter cold, long months of complete
darkness, constant danger, safe return doubtful.
Honor and recognition in case of success.

I imagine the Big Valley as a ship, bobbing through the year. We're about halfway to the safety of spring, but I am not a man, it isn't the early 1900s, and any chance I have at honor or recognition is laughable. There is no sea here, either, despite my active imagination; we are landlocked. The rest, though, sounds about right.

The boys and I have been lucky so far, and this has been a relatively mild winter, with some bone-bitter cold snaps but not a lot of snow—far less than the hundred or so inches we usually get. We've managed to keep an egress clear to the outside world by shoveling two long tracks in our driveway, from the Quonset hut all the way to the road, each track just wide enough for a vehicle's tires.

But some time last night while we were sound asleep that luck ran out. After two months of winter, we're finally socked in.

I've worked some long hours over the last two weeks on regular *Finding Utopia* projects, plus landed a few new freelance assignments, all of which require hard-copy edits and can't be e-mailed. I might not be anything close to an English knight on an expedition stuck on a frozen ship far from home, but I am a writer with finished work to deliver and get paid for; a mom with an empty refrigerator to fill with groceries I'll buy with the money; an adult with a gas bill and an electric bill so overdue they'll be shut off unless I pay them in person. Today.

Which I'll gladly do, just as soon as I can make it off this terrestrial iceberg.

And here's the crazy thing. Thundersnow is so rare that years, and sometimes even whole decades, pass without a single incidence of it. Then again, years pass without horses being panicked out of their secure pasture, without the unemployment rate climbing into the teens, without pig viruses mutating into a human flu, and without once-reliable freezers dying in the anonymity of their dark basements.

And certainly years pass without all of these misfortunes arriving at the same family's doorstep within just a few months of each other. This, I think, drinking my coffee and watching the light begin to reveal the entirety of just how snowed in we are, just isn't one of those years.

"Everything happens for a reason," Mr. Wonderful likes to say.

"No snowflake ever falls in the wrong place," a Zen saying goes.

"The Lord must have wanted it that way," Grandma Link used to say.

But it's February, it's winter, it's Michigan, and I don't believe any of it. I believe things just happen, and are neither good nor bad, but human beings are so hungry to believe in something that we try to make meaning out of random events. Especially the bad ones. We look for any good we can find in the hard stuff, hoping it will make us feel better, especially when we've got places to go, money to collect, and bills to pay. And sometimes, while we're looking, we're wearing snow boots and a wool hat and armed with a rusty snow shovel.

I let the boys sleep in and go outside and shovel the snow away from the door and partway down our brick walkway. I see what we're dealing with now and know the boys are going to need the extra rest, and don't wake them up until 8:30, when the thunder and lightning have passed. They come downstairs to the warm-butter smell of a pancake breakfast. There's still no sign of Jesus' face in any of our pancakes, but I've set the table, put out the butter, cut up the bananas, warmed the maple syrup, and even poured the orange juice.

If there are two words I could say that would please them more first thing on a February morning than "snow day," I don't know what those words would be. But if there are two they dread hearing more than "snow shovel," I don't know what those would be, either.

It's full daylight outside when I utter the latter, gesturing toward the window. My pajama-clad snow-removal team stands together, bellies full, and takes a good long look outside, sighting down on exactly what we're dealing with.

"Oh, rats," Will says, putting his own two words in.

"Thanks for the carbo load," Owen adds, seeing right through my elaborate breakfast. Luke is already dressed and heading for the mudroom, where we keep our coats, snow pants, hats, and gloves.

After his brothers get dressed too, the team and I suit up, boot up, man up, and head outside. We choose our weapons from the bent, cracked, and rusty options I keep jammed, handle first, into the snowbank that edges the walkway. There's so much snow and it's so heavy and wet that it takes us ten minutes of digging just to get the gate open so we can wrestle with the driveway.

Which, up close, gives us all pause. A lunar landscape of white stretches for what seems like infinity in front of us.

I plan a strategy while my sons stare at their bleached-out day. Feet stuck in drifts, holding their shovels at the ready, they are like a winter chain gang waiting for instruction. With my dark sunglasses, I feel like their chain-gang boss, mean and weary. I size up the job and just hope that my mysterious genetic heritage doesn't destine me for an early heart attack, stroke, or brain aneurysm. Because this is going to tax our systems.

"This is going to take us all day," Owen predicts.

"What, you have a prior engagement?" I snap.

"No. But snow days are supposed to be days off."

So they are. And refrigerators are supposed to be full, houses are supposed to be warm, and college-educated mothers with half a brain in their heads are supposed to be able to figure all this shit out. Everything happens for a reason? Whatever.

"Owen and Luke, you guys take one side, I'll take the other side, and Will, you clean up what we leave in the middle. Let's start at the garage and work our way to the road. Don't try to shovel it all at once, because you'll just get tired faster. Take it in small scoops."

That is the way we accomplish everything: in small scoops. That's the way we stocked up on squash and froze extra vegetables, that's the way we've kept the fireplace stocked with wood, that's the way I've grown, gathered, and bought our food, and that's the way we will get this driveway shoveled.

It takes us more than five hours. Our hearts are banging in our chests and we're out of breath, all sweaty and hot by the time we finish even though it's barely twenty degrees outside. But we clear every inch of our driveway out from under all that snow. We stand together at the end, where the driveway exits to the road, look back at our work, and catch our breath.

And for the first time in a long time, I'm proud of us. Proud enough even to balance my camera on the flat hood of the farm truck, set the automatic timer, and take a picture. Looking at the image, at my sons' faces, I'm pretty sure that they're proud of themselves, too. My memory of this day is dominated by smiles, by the sound of thundersnow, as well as the sense of heaviness that pressed down upon the morning.

But for once, something from that blasted SMILE handbook feels more like acknowledgment than judgment. "Parents are role models for children and need to set a good example for them. Children imitate the behaviors and attitudes of their parents."

If I can model hard work, that will at least be something.

With the job over, we are ravenous in a way that comes only after spending long hours outside in the cold. The warm air inside the house hits our stomachs, and those pancakes are just burned-up fuel. There's not much food in the house, and so the boys eat Jethro-sized bowls of cold cereal and milk.

I deliver my writing and editing work, cash the checks, pay the bills, stop at the grocery store and buy two bags of groceries. Pulling into the driveway, I make a stop for the mail. Bills—of course—and something else I actually look forward to receiving this time of year: three vegetable-seed catalogs. In the heaviest white glare of an endless winter, they promise that the colors of spring and summer still exist somewhere in the future.

While I'm gone on my errands, Owen finishes that history report—the one about Sir Ernest Shackleton. The snow day has given him some bonus time to finish it; he's used that time well, and his report is pretty good. I read it over when I get home and am reminded that even though it took Sir Ernest nine long months, he saved all of his men from what was thought back then to be certain death in the ice.

"Caution, perseverance, reckless courage, and strong idealism were his leading characteristics," according to Owen's research.

My son ends his report in the logical spot—with the once-triumphant explorer's death. Despite the man's long-shot heroics, and his years spent in the coldest, most remote and inhospitable places on earth, he didn't freeze to death or starve. He died of a heart attack, on board his comfortable ship, which was safely docked in port. He was probably even looking forward to spring.

9

March 2006

ECLIPSE

A total solar eclipse is probably the most spectacular astronomical event that most people will experience in their lives. Observing the sun, however, can be dangerous if the proper precautions are not taken.

—NASA SOLAR ECLIPSE BULLETIN, MARCH 2006

I am a winner. As unlikely as this seems, a radio announcer tells me it's actually true. On a weekend the boys are with their father I am listening to the classic-rock station in the afternoon, volume up real loud, drinking wine straight from the bottle, standing at the window, and watching it snow. When prompted by the deejay, somewhere perhaps between Van Halen and Heart, I pick up the phone and call in and am informed that I'm a winner.

My prize? Two tickets to see Uncle Kracker and his band that night at our area's one and only nightclub.

This is completely out of character for me. I have won things before, but always by skill and never by luck. I win tournaments at the local pool hall and even some that are held in large conference rooms far out of town that I carpool to on weekends that the boys are with their father. The prize money is enough to buy each of my sons a new pair of snow boots. I win a few honorable mentions in writing contests, some even with money attached. My divorce hearing is in a few days, so soon I'll know whether or not I'll win in court when my house and my children are at stake. But I do not win at luck—not ever.

And I do not call radio stations, either. Not to request songs and not to win prizes, yet here I am, in possession of two tickets to a sold-out performance of Uncle Kracker.

And another thing I do not do, *ever, ever, ever,* is ask men out on dates. I just don't do that.

In middle school, I wait as my mother decrees that boys have to call me, and not the other way around. In high school, when my boyfriend finds Jesus and refuses to take me to the senior prom, inviting me to a prayer meeting instead, I do have the wherewithal to tell him to cram it, but I don't call up any of our school's unattached jocks. I wait for one of them to hear the news that I am open and call me. The first one who does is my prom date.

Winning at luck must have changed my perspective, though, or else it's the wine, because I call up Pete the builder and offer him one of my free tickets. He can go with me if he wants to, or he can just take the ticket, go, and have a good time on his own or with someone else. I give him an out.

I've only spoken with him a handful of times since meeting him at that bar last fall, but I do still think of him often, and there's no one else I'd rather go to the concert with. What I actually say to him in my big moment is: "You don't have to go with me, I just thought you might want the free ticket." Aphrodite, we have established, I am not.

"How about if I meet you there?" he suggests.

Clairvoyant, I think, the way he senses my inner conflict. Either that or he is just as ambivalent about the prospect of the two of us out on a date as I am. I know he is the father of two sons, and I know he is estranged from their mother, but I know little else about his romantic life.

Maybe Pete isn't even attracted to tall, big-boned women with smart mouths and brassy hair. For all I know, he prefers petite girly-girls. In which case, I'm out of luck. Raised as the only daughter of a tomboy mother, I've made it past my fortieth year knowing very little about applying makeup, walking in high heels, layering, the suitability of plaids, or eyebrow shaping. I like clothes, and even have a twisted, voyeuristic love for fashion magazines, but I don't have any idea how to assimilate what's in style.

Both money and time are lacking for this pursuit, which seems to require a pile of each to do well.

But Pete has agreed to meet me at the concert, and actually sounded happy about the prospect. The boys won't be home until tomorrow afternoon and a half hour before my half date it's time to make myself look feminine. If that's even possible.

I start at the top, with my hair, which used to be a perfectly respectable dark brown. Then, in a moment of pre-menopausal hysteria, or post-thirtysomething showboating, or both, I went blond on my fortieth birthday. I don't mean that I got a few high-lights. I don't mean that I went a shade lighter than natural. No, I mean that I went full-on sunflower-and-chardonnay, honey-and-butter, slap-my-ass-and-call-me-Judy blond.

Before the split, I'd been maintaining my color for four whole years. Now, I haven't had a hair appointment in four months, and boy, does it show! But I've plaited it in more than a dozen small braids as a kind of follicular camouflage to hide the dark roots. Standing in front of my bathroom mirror, I take out the rubber bands one by one and then use my fingers to comb out the braids. With my height, my prominent shoulders, my dark eyes, and my obviously dyed hair, I'm a little concerned that this style will inspire comparisons to Dennis Rodman, but it actually turns out okay.

Now for the hard part—clothes and makeup. I put on mascara, cherry-flavored ChapStick, my favorite pair of jeans, a dusty-blue tank top with sequin trim (this may actually be something called a camisole, I'm not really sure), and over all this I plop on the garment so distinctive my sons have given it a name—Ugly Brown. This cabled and shapeless sweater is usually sitting vigil on my desk chair or tied around my waist, and tonight I find that I don't want to leave the premises without it.

This get-together with Pete is not really an official date, anyway, I tell myself. So there's no real reason to be nervous. It's just a—what does Owen call it?—a meet-up. A casual night of live music and fun.

It's only much later that I learn Pete is not anything close to an Uncle Kracker fan. That he likes his rock music harder and darker. That he would actually prefer listening to, say, Lawrence Welk sing about his bubble machine accompanied by a thousand accordions than listen to Uncle Kracker live, but that he wanted to see me, and if that meant enduring "Follow Me" at high decibels, he was willing to make the sacrifice.

I don't know this, though, when I head out into my driveway

with my rockin' hair and my sequined camisole and my pointy-toed ankle boots that are castoffs from a friend and a half size too small, but free.

And I'm almost to my minivan when a flash-freeze of wind aims itself right at me like a stun grenade. According to the calendar it is the middle of March, and winter is supposed to be on the downslope, but just try telling that to the weather. I angle my torso like a ski jumper, arms tight to my sides, and enter the whipping snow. Ugly Brown is flapping away in this gale that feels like it's been saving up since somewhere over the western prairies just to blast me and my little acreage. While I've been inside getting ready, this wind has sculpted snowdrifts in front of my door, next to my farm truck, and over the hood of my minivan.

The distance from my garage door to the end of my driveway is about half the length of a football field, but I can see that the road itself is pretty clear and it's just my driveway that looks like a scene from *Dr. Zhivago*.

If I can just ram my way through fifty yards of oscillating three-foot snowdrifts, the ones that seem to have arms reaching out for unsuspecting and preoccupied women like me, I'll be fine.

Because here's the deal. Once I'm driving down the road toward the nightclub with my two free tickets, I'll be out on the town on a Saturday night as a single woman with plans to meet someone of the opposite sex for the first time since, no lie, the Reagan administration.

I skip the minivan tonight and decide to take the farm truck instead. It chugalugs the gas, but it also has beefy tires and four-wheel drive, making it a better hedge against all those icy drifts now standing between Pete and me. And it's not until my gloved hand is on the door handle that I notice how well my hair's brown roots, and my brown ankle boots, and my Ugly Brown sweater all color-coordinate with my transportation option of the evening, my farm truck, "Cookie."

As much as I eschew signs, omens, and snowflakes in particular places, this unplanned symbiosis of earthy hues is a development I interpret as containing *a deeper meaning*. Okay, a sign. I am certain now that I was right to ask Pete to accompany me tonight because my hair has brown roots, I'm wearing a brown sweater, walking in brown boots, and getting into a brown truck. Hey, if everything is random, then you'd better just go on and grab some meaning wherever you can find it.

A blizzard in such a serendipitous circumstance as this seems like only a minor inconvenience.

Cookie rams the biggest driveway snowdrift head-on at 25 mph. That's as much speed as I can muster, stomping my pointy-toed boot on the accelerator and jamming the stick shift into second gear, but it's not enough. My truck lodges in the snowbank, both front tires half-buried and spinning.

And of course I know not to gun the engine. Anyone who learned how to drive in a snow state knows not to gun the engine when you're stuck in a drift. Especially when you're in a hurry. Because you'll only make it worse.

And I can't believe I'm actually stuck in my own driveway, because just think of the good luck that has gotten me this far. It has taken the hands of fate striking the hour of destiny on the solar system's great cosmic clock, what with the calling of the radio station and the winning of the tickets and the asking of the man. And now I'm going to be felled by something as pedestrian as the *weather*? I don't think so.

Maybe I am this excited about the prospect of being out on

a date with Pete. But maybe I just want to be a girl again for one night. *Please, God, let me do that one little thing.* Then I'll go back to being a broke, single, underemployed, man-hating mom. A statistic. But just for one night I'd really like to dance and listen to live music and drink and have some actual fun with another adult. A male adult.

I thought I'd followed all of the intricate steps necessary, in their proper order, to make this spontaneous moment happen. Now this.

I look up, as if by some miracle of spiritual physics my frustration could penetrate Cookie's roof, and say a prayer. *Sir or Madam,* I mouth to the concave brown Naugahyde upholstery overhead, and whatever, whoever, is beyond it. *Please let me get out of my driveway. Please. Because do you really think men like Pete are a common occurrence? Do you really think you scattered them all over your frozen creation down here like pinecones or something?*

And then I gun the engine. And maybe I gun it again, putting both feet on the accelerator this time, just for that teensy-weensy bit of emphasis.

Cookie's roof says nothing in return, but her front tires respond to the accelerator accordingly. They grind themselves deeper into the drift until her wheel wells are packed with snow and the sickening, ratcheting, wind-up sound of rubber on ice reverberates through the cold.

It takes me almost half an hour of working with the snow shovel and the pointed spade I fetch from the recesses of my garden shed to get free. I arrive at the nightclub Streeter's and park what seems like miles away from the door because I'm so late and the place is so packed that it's the only spot I can find. After a trudge across the frozen tundra of the parking lot, I am sweating mascara and my hair looks like I did the Polar Plunge into a pool of slush.

How do other single people manage? Is a date really worth all this trouble? This is what I'm thinking when I see Pete, standing in the crowd that is milling around outside, and he is smiling my way.

"Wow, you look great!" he says, actually seeming to mean it. Which indicates one of two things: he is either legally blind and has failed to mention it, or he likes me as much as I like him and so doesn't even register that I look like, and have the disposition of, a drowned blond wolverine.

And then we are inside, and even though it's open admission Pete scores us two great seats on the mezzanine that circles the dance floor, and Uncle Kracker comes onstage, and he's smiling and good-looking, and he starts to sing and his band sounds great.

After a few songs I see the real-estate agent who sold me my farm and she walks up to my seat and tries to pull me onto the dance floor and Pete motions to go ahead, he will save our seats. He will keep an eye on Ugly Brown because I am all camisole now, all faded jeans and vodka.

I'm dancing with a circle of women, some I know but most I don't, but it doesn't matter that my feet are still squishing inside my snow-soaked boots, because we are women without a worry or a care, all grinning one big grin. Yes, I think, feeling a carefree sense of well-being I'd forgotten was possible, it *is* worth it. Just to feel like this for a couple hours, it's worth the slush and the wind and the rubber bands.

Uncle Kracker is singing that everything is going to be all right and I want to believe him and he crouches at the edge of the stage and points down into the crowd for a minute and seems to point right at me. I look around, to either side of me, to the danc-ing women nearest me, and he laughs into the microphone while he's singing and points at me again.

My real-estate agent and her friends see this and simultane-ously release the universal rowdy-woman-pack cry "Woo-hoo!" into the night and we keep dancing and she leans in and shouts in my ear, "Cracker!"

The intimation is, of course, that you have to be a huckle-berryish, brassy country girl like me to attract the attention of a rocker named Uncle Kracker. For once my overly sensitive and politically correct self isn't even offended.

Next Pete and I dance to a slow song and his arms around me are plenty tight but they feel more like support than restraint and I'm not absolutely sure but I don't think that's the third vodka talking. Back at our seats, the looming real world creeps in as the alcohol wears off and I get quiet thinking about the week ahead.

My divorce hearing, by my rough calculations, is scheduled for forty hours from now.

The music is blasting as the band plays their last few songs so I think my mood blends in. I think that no one notices that the woman who was dancing and laughing earlier is sitting down and is quiet and moody now.

Pete touches my arm, though, wondering. "Everything okay?"

I look at him and start to smile, and start to yell, "Everything's great, everything's cool," but then I see his green eyes and that inquiring frown and feel the squeeze of his cabinetmaker's hand on my wrist and so for some reason instead, I just tell him the truth. Actually, I yell him the truth. As loud as I can, so I can be sure he'll hear me over the music.

"My divorce hearing is Monday!" I holler.

The band decides this is the exact second that their show is over and their song ends, and before most of the applause can erupt, my announcement reverberates across our section of the mezzanine. People turn and look at us, then laugh behind their hands, and I am mortified. What made me think I could date?

Pete says nothing, but his jaw goes a little slack in what I think is surprise and what I really hope is not embarrassment to be seen here with me.

"Let's go," he says, and with him leading and holding my hand we weave our way through the crowd and out into the parking lot We walk between the parked cars in the general direction of my truck, not really in any hurry despite the cold.

"Hey, I want to show you something," he says, his voice low. "What do you think?" He gestures toward an old pickup truck we're now standing next to. I give it the once-over and see that it is a sibling or at least a first cousin of Cookie, except that it's all white instead of two-tone brown.

"Of what?" I say.

"Of the truck," he says.

His regular ride is a royal-blue pickup, a newish one with cloth seats that he keeps scrupulously clean and waxed year-round. He also owns a plow truck and has told me all about the classic Mercury Comet he's restoring. This white junker he's pointing to is a little rusty, a little raggedy, and old.

"I just bought it this week," he says, listing all of the work it needs—brakes, a new hood, new ball joints (whatever those are)—as if these are all valuable attributes. There's even a crack running halfway across the bottom of the windshield. This truck is what we call a "winter beater"—a cheap but tough vehicle you drive in the winter because you don't care if it gets beat up by salt, snow, ice, bad drivers, snowplows, or suicidal deer.

"Guess what I named it?"

"I have no idea."

"Cracker," he says, nodding in emphasis, as if this should please me. Maybe the name is in homage to the singer we just listened to, but I don't think so, and he has to explain the name to me.

"It's the same make and year as your truck. You've got Cookie and now I've got Cracker. You're the writer. I figured you might appreciate the *irony*." This last word he enunciates as if it is on a vocabulary list and he has to use it in a sentence in order to get the extra credit.

"Are you making fun of me?" I ask, smiling now.

"Nope," he answers, deadpan, "but it didn't hurt to ask."

And that's how our meet-up, half date ends. Cookie and Cracker head off into the blowing and drifting winter night in two different directions. No kiss, no plans to see each other again, just a shared automotive bond—something, despite being born in the Motor City and spending the majority of my life in the most car-saturated state in the country, I've never experienced before.

The next morning my sons come back home, making the hundred-yard trek across the road, back to the Big Valley and up our plowed driveway right at noon. I'm a mother again, not a nightclub cracker, but I notice that the snowdrifts that were in my driveway are gone, the passage is clear now and lined with drag marks from a plow truck. Pete must have been here, plowed, and left before I even woke up. I can't think of anyone else who would plow my driveway without being asked. Or paid.

The boys are accompanied by their father, who shuffles along with them from his little rented place across the road, but only as far as the middle of my driveway, and then his shoulders slump and he turns back. I watch through the living room window as my beloveds walk these last steps alone: three refugees from the divorce war, trudging through the snow, returning to their frozen homeland.

I wonder what their father's house looks like on the inside, how the furniture, art, and the lamps we picked out together look arranged his way now, and in a whole new place. I'd like to know, but he has never invited me in to see. Not that that's enough to keep me out.

Because the next time I go to pick up the boys, Mr. Wonderful is not at home, and I'm invited inside the strange place by my sons and seize the opportunity to creep through the rooms like a burglar, noting the clean kitchen, the neatly folded laundry, and the dust-free bookshelves. In the midst of leaving us, Mr. Wonderful has somehow managed to make his emergency domicile, in a word, cozy, and it pisses me off.

Instead of being happy my sons have a nice place to share "parenting time" with their father, I'm disappointed that he's not suffering more. Guilt over this toxic feeling and the others I bear him will creep forward through the years like something darkly contaminated. It's sickening, and yet I can't stop myself from feeling it.

On the Monday morning after my date with Pete I gather the boys together at the kitchen counter. It is early, maybe 6:00, 6:15 a.m. Weekday mornings require split-second timing. There's homework to be checked, permission slips to be signed, string instruments for orchestra class to make sure are in their cases, and growing bodies to get bundled up and off to school. To accomplish this, I'm still getting up by five and they follow at six.

"Family meeting," I announce, and they groan but assemble dutifully at the kitchen counter and look at me with dread. In their experience, a family meeting is usually just an opportunity for additional chores to be meted out. To them, by me.

I've used family meetings to make weekly bathroom-cleaning assignments (three bathrooms, three boys: this is the kind of math I can handle), unveil a weekly chore chart, and give them snow-shoveling assignments. The agenda for this morning's meeting, however, has only one item on it and does not involve physical labor.

I'm dreading this conversation, and the four cups of coffee I've already downed, doubling my usual intake, are not helping. Silence engulfs the kitchen, penetrated only by the sound of my own leg's uncontrollable jiggling.

I take a deep breath, let it out, then inhale again. I try a simple mantra from my recent efforts at meditation. *Breathing in long, she discerns that she is breathing in long. Breathing out long, she discerns that she is breathing out long.*

"Um, okay," I say, taking in another breath, then exhaling again. "Well. So. Today is kind of a sad but important day."

Three sets of eyes stare right into mine, interested now despite the early hour. I don't do hesitancy, ever, at least not in front of them.

Breathe in, exhale.

If there were a Mardi mantra, it would go something like this: *Get on with it, you gutless wonder. Rip off that Band-Aid.* Repeat as necessary. But after another breath, I just blurt it out.

"Today is the divorce hearing. Today I'll go in front of a judge and he'll sign some papers from the lawyers and it will make everything official. After today, your dad and I won't be married anymore. We'll still be your parents, but we'll be divorced."

And then I do exactly what you're not supposed to do during meditation; I brace myself and hold my breath. I don't know what kind of reaction I'm expecting from them, but the boys just look at me for a moment, blink, and say nothing.

"Do you want to ask me anything about it?" I prompt.

Whatever ating I've expected is not forthcoming, though, and so instead of feeling relieved, I know right down to my anxious core that I deserve their wrath, their anger, or at least their disappointment in me, and I even have some pathological need to receive it.

Since not one of them offers this up freely, or immediately, I do my best to pry it out of them.

"Do you want to share how you feel?" I ask.

I am not unrewarded for my efforts this time. Owen stands up, shoves his stool in, and stomps upstairs.

"If you guys cared about your kids you wouldn't be doing this!" he shouts.

Luke follows quickly behind, his slim form soundless on the stairs next to Owen's pounding, not looking at me and saying nothing. He is the middle child off to do what he does best, make peace.

Will remains at the counter, frowning. I know this look. It's not an angry frown, it's an inquiring frown, a frown that means he's trying to figure something out.

"Mom?" he asks finally, lifting his head from where he's been resting it on his crossed arms. "Does everybody get their own lawyer when they're born? 'Cause I don't know who mine is, and what happens if I need 'im?"

He thinks that a conflict like the one between his father and me is a foregone conclusion. That this is what's in store for him: You grow up, you get married, you lawyer up, you get divorced.

If I had been standing, this lob of friendly fire would have cut me clean in half, but I'm sitting on an upholstered chrome counter stool directly across from him, trying to breathe, my midsection protected by kitchen cabinets.

"Lawyer is a job," I tell him, exhaling in a voice as even as I can make it. "Just like teacher or bus driver."

"Ohhhh," he says, and as this new concept crystalizes, the frown disappears.

"And if you play your cards right, maybe you won't ever need one."

"Well," he says, grabbing the strap of his backpack, "I only know Go Fish and Concentration, but Big Grandpa said he was going to teach me solitaire."

"Not with a Club, the Heart is broken / Nor with a Stone," Emily Dickinson wrote, "A Whip so small you could not see it / I've known."

Monday afternoon my whipped heart and I sit inside a courtroom at the Grand Traverse County Courthouse and I don't even bother and try to breathe. This is the moment I've been alternately wishing for and dreading for the last nine months.

My divorce lawyer is going over some paperwork with me. We're sitting at the back of the courtroom on a long wooden bench that resembles a church pew while up front the judge dispenses with the ruins of another woman's marriage. She is eighty years old if she's a day. At least I'm not her.

And then it's my turn, and the temporary custody arrangement Mr. Wonderful and I have been observing these last six months is made official and our possessions are divided. The one wrinkle is that my main form of transportation, our green minivan, will go to him. I'll be left with just the farm truck, which has only three seat belts, but I'll worry about that later. The good news is that I still have a shot at owning the Big Valley.

The judge gives me ninety days to refinance the farm in my name only. If I can't find a bank loony enough to lend me the money, I'll have to sell it, but this is not even an option in my world. Approaching a loan shark is an option. Joining a multilevel marketing scheme is an option. Selling twigs and berries on the Internet is an option. Ding-dong-Avon-calling is an option. My sons and I living anywhere but in our farmhouse together is not going to happen. I will find the money.

I wait for the gavel strike, but that is just a symptom of watching too many episodes of *Law & Order*. It never comes. Instead, the judge lifts his head from behind a stack of paperwork and takes off his Clark Kent–style eyeglasses.

"Good luck to you, miss," he says. It is only five words but he means them. Regardless of how many women he said these words to yesterday, or will say them to tomorrow, or the next day, or the day after that, when he says them to me I can tell he really means them.

It's the purely nicest thing a complete stranger will say to me all day, and maybe ever. He is not Clark Kent after all, he is Superman, his black robe a cape. That I feel such a huge pulse of gratitude for this small kindness only illustrates how alone I really am.

Exactly three months shy of my twentieth wedding anniversary, my marriage is severed.

Outside the courtroom I am heading for the stairway and home when I hear a familiar voice. It's coming from way down the hall and it rises above all the other voices in this high-ceilinged space and somehow cuts straight through the crowd and directly to my ear.

I like this voice, but wonder if it is an auditory mirage. Because it's Pete's voice I hear. And what would he be doing here?

"What are you *doing* here?" I ask him. He sees me but his smile doesn't disappear, it just grows wider as he lowers his head a little and shakes it slowly back and forth.

"My divorce," he answers.

"What?" I ask.

"My divorce is today, too. Right now. Any minute, actually."

I had been paying at least some attention to the woman whose divorce was immediately before mine, but haven't given one thought to whose divorce would come afterward. Strangely, this is like my fear of death, but in reverse. I worry about what will happen to my soul after I die, but give little thought to what it was doing before I was born.

On the wall is a locked document case that displays the day's courtroom schedule. Pete points at it. With my index finger leaving a sweaty, snail-like smear on the glass, I run down the day. There's "Mardi Jo Link vs. Mr. Wonderful," and right below it, "Pete vs. Mrs. Pete."

Each divorce hearing from 9:00 a.m. through 5:30 p.m. is listed by full name in twenty-minute increments on this schedule.

More than two dozen cases, and that's just for this one day. Somehow in this crazy and timeless universe, in this town of fourteen thousand, in this county of more than fifty thousand, where umpteen irreconcilable couples get divorced every year, Pete's divorce hearing and mine are scheduled in the same courtroom, in front of the same judge, one right after the other.

How is this even possible?

Coincidence, said Einstein, is God's way of remaining anonymous. I'm beginning to think this sockless, timeless mathematician might be onto something after all, because the very system designed to pull people apart is going against everything it stands for and inexplicably flinging Pete and me together.

In this moment of perfect earthly rotation, of serendipity, of good karma and divine providence all occurring on a day that should probably go down as one of the worst days of both in our lives, what do I manage to say to him? What pithy verbal response do I have to the fist of fate reaching down and clutching the two of us in its strong fingers and thrusting us together? What do I say to the man somebody up there somewhere thinks could be my destiny?

"Oh."

Do I sit down and wait for him? No. Do I smooth my skirt under my clenched behind and wait on the bench so I'll be the first friendly female face he sees after he officially becomes a single man again? No, I do not.

Instead, I run for the hills. For the stairs, for my doomed minivan, and for home. Romantic love doesn't exist for women like me. Time doesn't exist for anyone. And I need another man like Einstein needed a pocket watch.

Once through the door, I totter to my flowered chair, curl up, and snivel and sleep until the sound of the air brakes on the first of the school buses that will stop at the end of our driveway penetrates my stupor at four o'clock. Because our driveway is so long I've got a minute or two between when the school-bus doors open and the kids bust inside, and I'm at the sink splashing water on my face by the time Luke and Owen walk in the door.

"Hi, guys!" I sing, certain I'm presenting the face of a happy, albeit dripping, mother to them, the face of a woman to whom nothing much out of the ordinary has happened to today, or happens to any day. A mom focused on the second that her children will finally be home from school and the meaning in her life will resume.

I've already told them that the divorce hearing was today, they don't need a play-by-play of how it went. And, to be honest, I don't feel like talking to them about it ever again. I just want it behind us.

"How was school?" I chirp, as the boys walk out of the mudroom and into the kitchen, where I'm rummaging through cupboards for their after-school snack.

"What's wrong with your eyes?" Luke asks.

Now that I think about it, they do feel a little swollen. And they're burning, which means they're also bloodshot. I have Irish eyes. Big, brown, and tender. A couple good teardrops from way down deep can swell them half shut like they've been bee-stung.

"Remember?" Owen says before I can answer. "We're the divorced kids now."

10

April 2006

EGG MOON

Consider the Araucana. Few chickens are as delightful, especially if you have children, as the so-called "Easter egg chicken." They lay light bluish or greenish eggs, often resembling dyed Easter eggs. Remarkably, these eggs are blue even on the inside of the shell.

—*Farmers' Almanac*

Spring has got to be around here somewhere. I feel like I can't take one more second of winter, of cold, of darkness, of endings. And so, regardless of what the thermometer says, three days before Easter I have the boys pull our old metal porch furniture out of the garage. They wash the caked-on dirt and crispy ladybug shells off with a bucket of hot, soapy water and then arrange the chairs and the matching table on the porch.

It is an unseasonably warm evening, maybe forty degrees, bright and clear, and when I take a deep breath, the air is still cold but it really does smell like spring. Like bird nests and crocus blooms and dirt thawing out. Like fresh starts.

Everywhere there is the sound of dripping. Snow from eaves, ice from tree branches, snowbanks melting into the pond. Our driveway is completely clear and the low-in-the-sky sunshine slowly dries the porch chairs off. Even though it is still too cold to sit outside, I bundle up in a blanket and do it anyway.

This vintage purple porch set once belonged to my grandma Link, she of the Emergency Steak and the blood sausage and the Lutheran resolve. After her husband, my grandfather, died, she lived another three decades alone, and about this time of year she would grab these chairs single-handedly, ham-fisting them out of her garage, wipe them down, and set them up in her driveway. Whatever resourcefulness I have, I probably owe at least some of it to her. She taught me self-reliance through her actions, not her words, though I didn't always realize it at the time.

Because when you're twelve years old and you go stay with your recently widowed grandmother for a week in the summer, and she tells you that the scrumptious "fried chicken" you've just downed a whole plate of is actually a fat rabbit—maybe wild, maybe someone's escaped pet—that she caught that day in her backyard, skinned, disemboweled, and dropped, piece by floured piece, into boiling lard, "Wow! Isn't Grandma resourceful?" is not the first thing that pops into your head.

But in these first few days of spring, putting healthy food on our table is still a challenge for me. It was probably a challenge for her, too, I just didn't realize it. Remembering my grandma Link so clearly today has made me wonder if, even beyond those "Meat-Stretchers" in her old cookbook, we are missing out on another food source. I shun lard, and I'm pretty sure I couldn't bring myself to kill and dress a rabbit, even the ones who wiggle into the garden, but could I wring a chicken's neck? Maybe.

Even if I can't stomach plucking and gutting one, if we had our own flock of chickens at least we'd have fresh and free eggs. That'd be one way to replace the protein from Rocky. No killer instinct is required to scramble, poach, fry, or boil.

And so on Easter Sunday, when the Congregational church we are visiting sings a rousing version of "Jesus Christ Is Risen Today," I decide something important. The boys and I are going to try raising chickens. That hymn is probably supposed to inspire thoughts more pious than poultry, but an inspiration is an inspiration, even if mine comes with chicken feathers instead of angel wings.

Tractor Supply, the farm store a few miles south of us, is closed on Easter, and it's almost a week until I have time to get there on the following Saturday. I am a regular customer here, as regular as my budget allows, carting out dog food, soil thermometers, garden gloves, and mole traps. This is where I used to buy Rocky's hog chow and where I used to buy Major and Pepper's horse dewormer.

A department store for farmers the week after Easter is an unlikely place to experience a spiritual revelation. But after all of my Buddhist reading and our sporadic church visiting, I do know how precious spiritual moments are in my everyday life. If one arrives in the livestock department at Tractor Supply, well then, so be it.

I walk past the pallets stacked with fifty-pound bags of goat chow and the rows of new John Deere lawn mowers. I glance at the bargain bin of tools and move toward the racks of vegetable seeds but pull myself away before I start fondling the packets of haricots verts or black-seeded Simpson. I make a mental note instead: time is running out on ordering from the seed catalogs I have back at home, the ones stacked on top of the bill file.

The Holy Grail I'm seeking today, though, is the help desk in the back of the store, where a man named Larry presides like the Pope—the Pope of farming.

I don't know Larry's last name and he doesn't know mine, but from him I have learned any number of useful skills: how to estimate the amount of electric fence needed for a two-acre pasture (measure, then multiply by three); what the secret is to growing mammoth pumpkins (pinch off all the early blossoms but one); and a surefire repellant for Japanese beetles (squish their kin, float the dead bodies in a bucket of dishwater, and place strategically).

I've followed each of these suggestions like the good little agricultural acolyte that I am. They all work. Larry is a real farmer, not a wannabe like me. He is the son of a farmer, the grandson of a farmer, and the great-grandson of a farmer. I am the daughter of schoolteachers. He has hundreds of acres and hundreds of head of cattle to match. He is a judge for the 4-H, butchers his own pigs, can surely do the big "S" himself, and probably not with a handgun, either. I have a farmhouse and six acres that my sons and I are still hanging on to, miraculously, by our dirty fingernails.

I have a *Wayne's World* moment every time I approach the help desk and see Larry in his sporty red TSC vest standing behind it: I'm not worthy. But I am something better: ready. Ready to try something new but practical. Something docile and inexpensive and not so big that I can't consider killing it, or so cute that we can't eat it. Like chickens.

The boys like the idea, too. I talked to them about it on our way home from church on Easter, and I could tell by their enthusiastic responses that they are fully vested.

"Boys," I announced, "we're going to raise some chickens."

"Another pet to play with!" said Will, the idealist.

"Another kind of poop to clean up," said Luke, the worker.

"Another animal in bondage," said Owen, the activist.

"Rule over all the livestock on earth," said God, the God.

Ostensibly, God said this to "man" in the first chapter of Genesis, but what if Adam was off somewhere taking a toke on his bong; then wouldn't these directives be settled upon Eve? I mean, there was no one else around, right?

Although I have been without a husband for ten months, and although my spiritual searching began about the same time, I am so raw still, so unevolved spiritually, that with spring and Easter on my mind, Genesis actually feels like a pretty good place to start.

I don't know about ruling over livestock, especially since I still believe that I am to blame somehow for what happened to Major, and for what happened to Rocky's meat, but I still think I can handle chickens. I don't tell any of this to Larry, of course. When I take my turn at the help desk, I'm all business.

"I want to buy some chickens," I tell him. "How do I do it?"

Larry has come to expect all my questions to have a "how?" in there somewhere, and he reaches under the counter, pulls out a thick, four-color catalog, opens it up, and right then it feels like the whole earth downshifts in slow motion. The age-old chicken-and-egg question becomes immaterial. Chickens—and if you want them, fertilized eggs, too—come from the post office. The way to buy chickens is through mail order.

"Good thing you came in today," Larry says. "It's the last week for orders, and the hatchery is closed on Sundays."

I look up at him, at his scratched eyeglasses, his pocked and bluish nose, and at that moment I am aware of my surroundings: Larry's wisdom is an immediate blessing, and I think he might be the most enlightened being on earth.

Chickens from a catalog. On a Saturday.

You can order up the birds on the sixth day of the week, just like God ordered up all the animals on *the* Sixth Day.

It surprises me to consider the previously unthinkable possibility that in the months since I lost the horses, the Big Valley has actually grown closer to being a real farm, and not, as I feared, farther away. A real farm feeds the people who live on it, and we are working toward this.

I would definitely not have expected the way toward this realization to wind through Tractor Supply, but I am trying to let go of my expectations. I am getting back to basics, and what could be more basic than an egg?

I look back at the catalog. There are light-brown chickens and black-and-white-striped chickens. There are chickens with fancy feathers cresting the tops of their heads and chickens so small they look like quail. There are even chickens that look like celebrities. Foghorn Leghorn, the Kellogg's Corn Flakes rooster, and Nathaniel Hawthorne's Chanticleer. In each vivid rendering, a rooster and a hen are shown, the rooster erect and proud, throwing out his chest, the hen calm and plain and friendly looking.

"Meat or egg?" Larry asks me.

"What?"

"What d'ya want, meat chickens or egg chickens?"

He says this quietly, and with the patience of a kindergarten teacher, even though there are three people in line behind me.

Which came first, chicken stir-fry or egg foo young? Barbequed chicken or deviled eggs? I don't even have the birds yet and I already feel inadequate. I still haven't decided if I'm going to kill them or not, and I had no idea meat chickens and egg chickens were two different birds.

Everything, I learn later, depends on that decision. What kind of feed you buy, what kind of coop you build, how long you plan on keeping them, and how they will get from coop to stove.

Under the watchful eyes of Larry, I decide not to decide and tell him, Eve-style, that I want both. I want it all. He nods, almost as if he were expecting this to be my answer. This is called a "mixed run." A straight run is all hens, also called pullets. The hens, the girls, are more expensive. I'm not sure why that is, but I like it.

"Okay, now you gotta pick your breed."

"Hmmm" is all I can muster.

Larry suggests Leghorns for my meat chickens and Ida Browns and Araucanas for my egg chickens. All three breeds can tolerate the northern Michigan cold. Before he closes the catalog and puts it back under the counter, he tells me there's something else.

"Them Araucanas are called the 'Easter Egg chicken' because their eggs are light blue and light green. Ain't that something?"

Can it get any more spiritual, I wonder, here among the galvanized toolboxes and salt blocks and rolls of chicken wire? I place a minimum order—ten egg and fifteen meat. They are $2 each for the mixed run, $2.75 each for the straight run of hens. I write a check out of my *Finding Utopia* money for $57.50 plus tax and shipping. Not a bad deal for a Saturday-morning revelation.

Seeds are much cheaper than chickens, but their catalogs are just as glorious. Some women might drool over designer clothing, lingerie, or home-decorating catalogs but I reserve my coveting for the catalogs that offer mail-order vegetable seeds. These companies have names like Nature's Crossroads, Abundant Life, the Cook's Garden, Johnny's, and Fedco. I order only organic seeds from companies based in the Midwest or at least from places in cold-weather climates. A tomato from Texas or a bean from Alabama is probably not going to make it here.

A small fire glows in our fireplace and I spread the catalogs out on the dining room table. Outside there is still snow on the ground and the trees are bare, even though a few patches of grass are showing near the old stone foundation of the house. It's hard to believe that it will ever be warm enough to grow the heat-loving melons and gleaming purple-black eggplants that take some coaxing to ripen in our short season, but these catalogs, and my own experience, assure me otherwise.

The Congregationalists have the Bible to refresh their faith; I have seed catalogs.

Color photographs of Ox Heart tomatoes, Jacob's Cattle beans, Tall Telephone peas, and Detroit Red beets beckon. I love the vintage names people have given these heirloom vegetable seeds over the years, some of which are old favorites that have been grown in American gardens for a century or more.

That history makes me feel connected to a whole ancestry of farmers and gardeners I labor alongside of through time, but will never meet or know. It makes me feel part of something bigger than me, bigger than my sons, bigger even than the Big Valley. All of which will, if I take care of them, still be here on this earth long after me.

I see something called an Eight Ball zucchini and have to order some, just for the name. This is a tiny extravagance: a packet of seed is only $1.50.

There's poetry, too, in the catalog descriptions. Fedco's are my favorite. Their catalog is just tiny black-and-white text and a few drawings, no photographs, so maybe that's why they put so much obvious love into the writing. A radish's "crisp white flesh has a good sweet taste with only a little heat." And here's to Presidential leeks, a relative of the onion: "Lincoln may be sown thickly like scallions, and bunched for discerning chefs. Will withstand frosts." Be advised, however, that yellow tomatoes "will catface under cold or excessively wet conditions."

And I learn new things from these catalogs, too. A parsnip pie is an amazing treat. The spicy burn in hot peppers is caused by a naturally occurring compound, capsaicin; police-issue pepper spray is made from this same chemical, just concentrated.

And if one has cause to order more than *fifty pounds* of Brussels-sprout seeds, there is a price break. I grow Brussels sprouts, too. A seed for this vegetable is the size of a small peppercorn, and I try to imagine the farm and the mother and the children who preside over such a harvest. They are superheroes.

A bush bean's varietal description from Fedco makes me smile, though, because I think it says as much about me as it does about the bean: "Nothing provides like Provider, even under adverse conditions."

I add three packages to my order: $6.10.

Because I've been busy ordering the chickens, planning the garden, ordering the vegetable seeds, and working for *Finding Utopia,* we haven't been to church in two weeks, not since Easter Sunday.

So far, we haven't found a place to call our church home, but I'm still determined to try. My grandma Link was a dedicated

Lutheran, and she attended the same church for more than eighty years. In her memory I rally the four of us to visit another new church this week.

I know what the Lutheranism of my childhood has to offer, and that's not exactly what I want to pass on to my own children, so this Sunday we give a nondenominational church a try instead.

Will needs no encouragement on this enterprise, Luke is neutral, Owen skeptical. Combined, their approach to organized religion mirrors my own. And even though I can still feel those Easter hymns inside me, the Congregationalist reverend's sermon about America's "just war" and the place for such an opinion in a church on Easter still irritate me, and we won't be going back.

We pick a new church to visit out of a newspaper ad. The ad is small and doesn't say much beyond the time of worship, but it does advertise that they are a flock known for their practical Christianity and their optimism, which both sound pretty good to me. I could be the poster woman for optimistic practicality, so when we sit down in folding chairs inside a gymnasium, I am hopeful our blind-date church will turn out to be "the one."

At the appointed time a tall woman wearing a caftan made out of wads of purple scarves sewn together twirls up to the lectern and chants a modern interpretation of a familiar Bible verse into a scratchy microphone: "But whoever takes the water I give him will never be in need of drink again, for the water I give him will become in him a fountain of eternal life."

Uh-oh, I think, *so it's* that *kind of church.*

Yes, this sermon turns out to be about the innate strength of all God's children to confront our nation's epidemic of alcoholism. There is emotional testimony from several members of the congregation and an overhead projector that flashes the times and locations of area AA meetings.

Owen and Luke sit next to me in our pew, and there's not a fidget in either one of them, stunned as they are into stillness by personal tales of Breathalyzers, jail-cell toilets, and other wayward stops on the long trek to sobriety.

For the first time I realize that my sons are the only minors in the room. And then Will, who said he wanted to try going into the Sunday-school classroom with the other kids his age, chooses this moment to return to my side.

"They got stuffed animals in there," he whispers, "And they smell like pee."

Before I can process this non sequitur, the woman in purple marches back up front. We should use the power of our minds and the power of the Bible's spiritual water to replace the rusty nails, the Bloody Marys, the sacramental wine.

I casually look to the left and right. People are watching her intensely, lowering their chins and praying, and even smiling and nodding their assent. Guilt, guilt, guilt is what I feel. How could I dare feel superior to these worshippers? They have all found their church home; my sons and I have not.

But still, this is not the thought process I was hoping to enter into for an hour by coming to church today. I was hoping to put my mind and my heart and my sons' souls in a place where we could explore the way I felt days ago inside Tractor Supply. I was hoping to learn how to find God in our everyday lives.

The woman in purple flounces off and a thin man with his skullet tied into a long gray ponytail begins setting out dozens of Tibetan singing bowls in a circle. He sits cross-legged in the center of them, moistens his fingertips in his mouth, and begins to "play" the bowls.

I look over at my sons, willing them with a silent maternal commandment not to laugh. Will can't slap his hands over his ears fast enough. Owen and Luke gawk openly, and I can't blame them. If I wanted to hear screeching like that, I could have gone out behind the barn and pumped the rusty well handle a few times.

Sitting in the back of this church was a brilliant move on our part, though, and the boys and I scoot out mostly unnoticed. And for the first time in months, I've worked up one heck of a thirst.

I stop at the grocery store on the way home and buy a half-dozen donuts for the boys and a half-pint of vodka and a bottle of tomato juice for me. Sunday brunch. They eat all the donuts without the least bit of difficulty, but I'm done for after just one Bloody Mary. I guess a tolerance for liquor, like faith, is something you lose if you don't exercise it at least once a week.

So far, our sporadic church field trips have been a bust. We haven't learned much, the time could have been better spent working, I'm drinking liquor on a Sunday just after the noon hour, and am no closer to nailing down the "What do I believe?" question than I was when we started. I feel like I'm responsible for my sons' souls too, not just my own. Someday, when they're older, I hope they ponder this question for themselves. But how will they do that if I don't give them somewhere to ponder it *from*?

My grandmother and my parents gave me their Lutheran beliefs: that hard work is practically a sacrament; that Jell-O is a perfectly respectable dessert to bring to a church potluck; and that the right way to sing hymns like "Stand Up, Stand Up for Jesus" is respectfully—and sitting down. Church is important, I learned from them, but that's no reason to get carried away.

I've rejected what feels like religious blandness. Far be it from me to frown down on anyone's emotional outbursts, but I have nothing to put in its place. Besides a respect for hard work, what spiritual legacy will I give my sons?

Of the precious moments of grace we've experienced over the past year—standing among prizewinning zucchinis, looking up at the stars during a winter campfire in the valley, decorating our Christmas tree, triumphing over thundersnow, ordering chickens from a catalog—not one of these moments has arrived when we've been inside a church.

My goal for the morning might have been spiritual connection, but my goal for the afternoon is something more down-to-earth: I've got to get the garden's irrigation system hooked up and tested. I refuse to let church or liquor get in the way of what's really important: water. Real water, and not the ethereal kind, either. The kind that irrigates your vegetables and that you control with a pump and a well.

It's only April, but if I want vegetables by late summer I need to get the seeds planted in early May, and if I want those seeds to germinate and grow, I'm going to need their water source to be operational before I plant them.

Every northern farmer and every gardener knows this: the time to start working toward a good fall harvest is in the early spring.

My irrigation system is not anything special, just a series of hoses, connectors, shutoff valves, and sprinklers that I take down, drain, and store in the shed every fall, then cobble back together again every spring. While not exactly photogenic or scientific, this system has three obvious advantages: it's cheap, the boys and I can put it together by ourselves, and it works. Once it's in place and calibrated correctly, I can water the whole garden by turning on just one valve.

"Let it rip!" I yell to Owen after we get everything laid out. He is stationed at the relay pump behind the barn. I can't see him from my spot just outside the garden fence, but I know he's lifted the arm of the pump, because a few seconds later a pathetic trickle of water streams out from the top of my oscillating sprinkler. This spray should blast out in a forty-foot circle, but it just pulses and sputters, wetting a pathetic ring in the dirt about the size of a birdbath.

"Shut it down!" I call.

I unscrew the sprinkler head from the post, slap it against my leg a couple times, and dead bugs flop out. Earwigs. I screw the sprinkler head back into its metal post, call out to Owen, and he lifts the pump arm up again. This time the spray goes about three feet. We wait a few minutes to see if the water pressure will build and extend the spray farther, but it doesn't.

For the next hour we check hoses, open and close valves, make sure all the water is turned off in the house, but to no avail. A three-foot stream of water with no more force than that of a school drinking fountain is all we're going to get without an intervention.

Over the past several months I've noticed a drop in our water pressure whenever I have the laundry and the dishwasher running at the same time. I think back to the boys running through the sprinkler late last summer and remember that it only spat out about half the spray that it used to. But I had plenty of other things to worry about back then, and chalked it up to a kink in the hose or an erratic electrical pulse going to the pump.

Those things were obviously not the problem. There's something wrong with the Big Valley's whole water system, not with the sprinkler, not with the irrigation system, and not with the relay pump. I keep telling myself that knowing how bad things are, admitting that there is a problem that needs attention, is better than not knowing, even when that reality turns out to be worse than I'd imagined.

But just because you repeat something to yourself over and over again doesn't make it true. The worst thing that can go wrong on a farm besides foreclosure or fire is a bad well. And the worst time for a well to go bad is in the spring. The established vegetable plants of summer can take a little drought and still grow. Maturity might be delayed, but the plants will still flower and produce. They can wait for rain. Seeds can't. If a seed dries out, it dies.

This is not like our heat problem, or our snow problem, or our food-supply problem. This is not something I can figure out how to fix myself, with an idea, hard work, my sons' help, and a little mental elbow grease. We *have* to have water, there's only one source for it, and beyond knowing how to climb down inside the well pit and jiggle the contact points on the pump when they ice over and short out, I have no idea how to fix a well. None.

"Whatcha got here is a wore-out pump, some corroded drop pipe, and a plugged screen," the driller I call on Monday tells me, climbing out of the well pit.

The pump and the drop pipe are at least sixty years old, he says, and the system is on its way to breaking down completely. When the pump was installed some time back in the 1940s or 1950s, three-quarters of a horsepower would do the job for a family. But this was before dishwashers or high-capacity washing machines or garbage disposals. Before daily showers or clog-free toilets. Because my well's infrastructure is such a geezer, and at the end of its life, the driller estimates it is only pumping water at the rate of three GPM—gallons per minute—or about as much water as a showerhead delivers.

"And missy, you can't irrigate a garden like the one you got planned out there with a showerhead."

We were just getting some traction, too. We made it through the winter, I've got work, warm weather is finally here, and the boys are thriving at school. Now this. Bad news isn't a stalk of corn or a green tomato: it doesn't get any sweeter with time. *Get on with it,* I think, returning to the Mardi sutra. *Rip off that Band-Aid.*

"Bottom-line me," I say to the driller.

We stand in silence next to the well pit while he calculates an estimate in his head. A new pump, sixty-seven feet of galvanized pipe, and a new stainless-steel screen for the wellhead, all fitted together by him with brass connecting hardware, is going to run me $2,325.00 and change.

This figure is too heavy for me to hold for long and drops in my gut like a boulder. He might as well have quoted me ten thousand dollars, a hundred thousand, a million.

My face must betray my panic, because the driller, a compact, kind-looking man in his sixties, looks down at his boots and makes a quiet suggestion.

"Maybe you'd like to talk it over with your husband."

My circumstances are so unsalvageable that even my I-am-woman-hear-me-roar self doesn't think to be offended by this. He is not being condescending, anyway, he's just being practical. Most couples I know wouldn't spend this kind of money without discussing it together first. My parents once had an agreement that neither of them would spend more than a hundred dollars without letting the other one know about the purchase.

"I don't have one," I say, just as Will opens the door to let me know that we're out of milk. Again.

"We're *always* out of milk," Luke grumbles from somewhere inside the house.

The driller watches this exchange, watches as Will looks hard at me for a second, says nothing, then ducks back inside and closes the door.

"How much can you pay today?" the driller asks, sighing.

My turn to do some calculating. If I pay the mortgage late, pay the other bills later, and use every cent of my *Finding Utopia* money earned in the past couple of weeks, I can pay almost a quarter of his estimate as a down payment.

The driller sighs, then nods, opens his clipboard, and hands me the carbon copy of the bill. Just another one to add to my folder. I read through it and see that $1,000 of his estimate is his labor cost. I know all about labor, and there's something that feels a lot worse about financing another working person's sweat than financing inanimate pieces of equipment.

My new Flint & Walling 1.5 horsepower deep well jet pump will be delivering 11+ GPM. "This means you can run three to four faucets wide open all day long!!" the driller has jotted down proudly. And, I think with relief, I can water all of our vegetable seeds. Those seeds will grow into the vegetables from the catalog photographs. Vegetables that we will eat.

This bill is handwritten on preprinted letterhead, with my name and address in the upper-left-hand corner, the date in the right, and this in fine print at the very bottom: "St. John 4:14: But whosoever drinketh of the water that I shall give him shall never thirst, but the water that I shall give him shall be in him a well of water springing up into everlasting life." I recognize it as the traditional translation of the same verse I scoffed at yesterday when the woman in purple read her version in church. Jotted above this verse on my bill is another absolute, this time in the driller's steady hand. "Note: There is a 1 Year Warranty on New Pump."

Barring a miracle, it is going to take me a lot longer than that to pay him off. But I will do it.

Time, my own tiny faith, the phases of the moon, and growing our own food are all sitting next to each other, not on a church pew but on one big continuum, spinning and spinning. My sons and I are just four small marks carved deep into some unfathomable cosmic wagon wheel, hanging on.

By the end of April all that remains of winter is a big pile of melting snow left over from Pete's occasional and "anonymous" snowplowing. The lawn is a greenish sponge, poppies sprout from the perennial border, and robins fly back and forth from the pasture to the lilac hedge, carrying little bundles of forgotten hay in their beaks. The migrating birds come back to the Big Valley, even though my bird feeders are still empty. There's no sign of Edgar, the injured green heron.

I'm deeper in debt for the well, but at least I will be able to water the garden we're getting ready to plant. To save money, I shut off the furnace. We're outside most of the time now, anyway, or the boys are at school. All we really need to stay warm are jackets, turtlenecks, long underwear, and a morning fire in the fireplace. That's the only time of day the house is still so cold.

"Tendernesses, / hesitantly, reach toward the earth / from space," Rilke wrote of this season, "and country lanes are showing / these unexpected subtle risings. . . ."

Most of my mail-order seeds have arrived and with the new well pump the sprinkler soaks the soil perfectly on my say-so. I like the idea of tenderness being expressed from above. Especially if it is expressed toward us, down here on our country lane, and I'm anxious to get my hands in the dirt again. The only harsh brown left anywhere on the Big Valley is, of all places, in the garden.

Winter broke down everything left over from last fall except some cornstalks, dry sunflower stems, and a trellis of ragged bean vines. Usually, these would have been composted over the winter, but last fall there just wasn't time to get the garden put to bed properly. With the promise of green surrounding as everywhere else, these plant husks stand guard over soil just waiting to envelop our recently arrived vegetable seeds.

This is my favorite thing about spring. It's the shortest season of all, sometimes there's barely enough time for a calendar page to slip between snow and summer, but it somehow manages to last long enough every year for me to clear out the old and start again.

I choose Will to help me with this task, since lately I've been depending so much more on his older brothers than I have on him. I've leaned on the two of them for help not just with the physical work, but with a lot of the emotional work, too. Time for Will to do his part.

I point to the garden, point to the stalks and husks and vines, then point to the compost pile.

"Do I *have* to?" he says, when I lay out the job.

Will is such a grumbler lately where hard work is concerned that I've devised a strategy just for him. If he accepts a chore cheerfully and completes it well, I release him from further responsibility and he's free to go about his day. He's free to build with Legos, make elaborate Matchbox racetracks down the stairs, set up his army-man wars, or build forts in the woods.

But if he complains, either when the job is assigned or during his completion of it, or if his work is subpar, I make him finish it properly and then I follow up with another chore—preferably a harder one that takes him even longer to complete. And here's the kicker: I don't say a word to him about this trick. And if he doesn't figure out what I'm up to, this could go on all day.

"How much are you paying me?" he asks, as we pull on our old boots and our work gloves.

"Same as I'm making," I tell him. "Zero dollars."

"Awesome."

That sarcasm just signed you up for another chore, buddy, I think, running through the options in my mind and plotting out what that next chore will be. *Picking up all the litter out by the road? Picking up all the dog crap in the backyard?*

"I can't believe I don't even get an allowance anymore," he says.

Okay then, dog crap it is.

I do have a reason for treating him this way. I want him to grow into a man unafraid of hard work. A man who approaches a challenge cheerfully and with resolve, no matter what that challenge is. A man who takes pride in the results for pride's sake, and not always because he's getting paid. I want work to be as natural to him as it is to me—something that's just a regular part of his day, whether it's caring for the dogs, shoveling snow, or putting the dregs of last year's garden into the compost pile.

If I have to trick him along the way in order to make that happen, so be it.

We work together for an hour or so, uprooting all the dead plants in the garden and tossing them next to the compost pile. I'm the lucky recipient of the silent treatment for about five minutes, but he is not the kind of boy who stays mad for long. He breaks up the cornstalks and sunflower stems into smaller pieces while I turn the compost pile with a pitchfork.

Steam rises from inside the pile. Will notices and comes over to investigate this by-product of healthy decomposition.

"Can I try?" he asks, holding his hands out for the pitchfork.

I hand it over smugly—my plan is working, he's into the task now—and he takes it from me in his boy hands, hefts it up and down a couple times, then hurls the tool one-armed deep into the center of the pile like a spear. His back arches like a gladiator's, fists raised to the heavens, his boy body in a compact Y. He roars the roar of victory, then turns to grin at me.

"Nice one," I say. "The worms are terrified. Now how about actually turning some of it."

The gladiator disappears, Will the boy returns, and goes to work on the pile. He digs and turns, digs and turns, making it about halfway through when something, or rather several somethings, flees his bayonet.

Our compost pile is home to crickets, spiders, worms, earwigs, centipedes, and every creeping thing that creeps on the earth according to its kind. Some of these creatures are completely unidentifiable without an entomology degree. And every time I turn the pile, they scramble out.

But these somethings Will has just uncovered have fur, not exoskeletal shells. They have whiskers, tiny round ears, and silky gray bellies. They have intelligent eyes—*panicked* intelligent eyes. They are meadow voles: a bigger, chubbier, and decidedly cuter relative of the mouse, with little round butts and stubs for tails and faces straight out of a Beatrix Potter illustration.

Will sees them too, drops the pitchfork on the ground, and bends down to get a closer look as the voles try to scatter. Some can't run at all, because they are just babies.

"I broke their house," he breathes out softly. "I broke their little house."

We comb through the warm earth and broken cornstalks and find a loose nest of grass, milkweed fluff, and hay. There are three babies curled together inside. They have fur, their eyes are open, but they don't look quite big enough to survive on their own. Will cups the nest in his hands and watches as they try to squirm away from the light.

"They're going to die now, aren't they?" he asks.

"Maybe," I answer.

We try to save them by digging a new hole in a corner of the garden, in the same area where the other older voles just ran. Will sets the nest of babies inside, then covers it with dead grass, more milkweed fluff, and a lattice of bean vines.

"People wreck everything," he says, standing now and looking at the results of our rescue effort. The hole is a little obvious, not well blended into our garden landscape the way it was when the voles built it themselves.

"They sure do," I say. "But people can fix things, too. You made them a good little nest. If we leave them alone, maybe the mother will come back."

Will looks at the nest and considers this possibility.

"If she doesn't," he decides, "they're goners."

We wipe down our tools and put them in the shed. I tell him

his work is over for the day. Who has the heart to make him clean up dog crap after this? I sure don't. I brought him into the garden this morning to teach him a lesson. One I thought he needed to learn—that he was overdue for, even.

I just didn't think it was going to be this one.

11

May 2006

FLOWER MOON

It's like being lost
in the forest, hungry, with a
plump live chicken in your cradling
arms: you want to savage the bird,
but you also want the eggs.

You go weak on your legs.
What's worse, what you need
most is the companionship,
but you're too hungry to know that . . .

—JENNIFER MICHAEL HECHT, "Chicken Pig"

It takes three weeks from the day I ordered our chickens until they arrive, but in May I get a call in the middle of the day from a clerk at the post office.

"Your chickens are here!" she says. "I've got them on my counter and they're peeping like crazy!"

I picture the full-grown chickens from Larry's catalog hopping and clucking around the post office. In this scene I conjure, they are pecking at the stamp machine and hopping onto the packages. They are scratching at the linoleum floor, looking for food. I've got to get over there.

Will's school is on the way to the post office, so I call Nurse Ratched and tell her I am on my way to pick him up and I'll be taking him out of school for the rest of the day. With such a stellar attendance record as his, this is unusual.

"Everything's okay, I hope?" she asks, probing.

"Everything's fine," I tell her, and leave it at that. I'm not going to give her the chance to ask me how the free lunches are working out.

When I get to the school, she already has Will sitting in the orange chair, and he looks at me, relieved, but his face is a question mark. I smile but say nothing, sign him out, and we walk out to our doomed minivan.

This will probably be the last time he rides in it with me, since I have to turn it over to his father. I choose not to think about that right now, though, because once inside, with the doors safely closed and all authority figures out of earshot, it is just the two of us in here together and I don't want to wreck it.

"Why are you here?" he asks me.

I relax into the present, and everything else disappears. This is the first time I have ever achieved this level of mindfulness, and Will's honest question fills me up so full, there's no room for anything else.

"The chickens are in," I whisper, as if we could still be overheard.

"Cool," he whispers back.

Right now, this second, I am not the woman who divorced his father, I am not an authority figure, I am an accomplice. I turn around and look at his still-small frame dwarfed by the big backseat. He is expectant. Innocent still, thank God. Surprises for him are always good ones. Time might be unreal, but this moment isn't. And inside of it is our past, our present, and our future, too.

So much of childhood fades; I want this to be a day he'll remember as an adult. I want this moment to be the way he remembers the whole of his growing up with me—unconventional, earthy, fun.

The post office looks normal enough: a line of people waiting to mail a package or a letter; three clerks at their windows helping customers. There is no evidence of a chicken infestation. Everything smells clean. Industrial. We get in line and soon are up at the counter.

"We're here to pick up our chickens," I say, as if this were the most common thing in the world.

"Right," the clerk says, index finger in the air, immediately heading to the back room. She returns with a box that is making high-pitched cheep-cheep-cheeping sounds. The box is very small, because—*duh, Mard*—they are baby chicks, not full-grown chickens. They must be very tiny, because twenty-five of them fit inside a container not much bigger than two egg cartons.

"Be careful when you open the box—it says the directions are under the shipping label."

Directions? She pushes the box toward me, our business concluded. I take it and we walk out the door and get into the van. I can't believe that they just let me leave. I'm being trusted with twenty-five innocent lives. I felt this way when I left the hospital after Owen was born. Are they really going to let me just take a newborn baby? What are they thinking? Don't they know I have no idea what I'm doing? In the backseat, Will holds the box on his lap and gently pushes his pinky through one of the airholes.

"They're pecking me!" he laughs. "They think my finger is a worm."

Once home, we take the box into the kitchen and open it up. Inside is a pile of yellow cotton balls with eyes. They look up at us in unison, then flock into a corner of the box. They're terrified.

"Eww!" Will says.

They stink. Bad. But this doesn't deter him from petting their fluff.

The directions are titled "Basic and Emergency Care for Baby Chicks." I do not want to consider any emergencies. The basics are this: Keep the temperature between 90 and 95 degrees for the first week, five degrees less per week down to 70 degrees. Keep chick starter—special food—available at all times. Provide water with three tablespoons of sugar per gallon mixed in for the first three days; dip the chick's beak in the water, because they may not know how to drink yet. Pray.

This last bit of advice does not appear in the written directions, but I think it should. Their bodies are so fragile, my barn has been empty for so long, and it is drafty and big.

We put the lid back on the box, leave the chicks on the kitchen counter, and drive back to the source, Tractor Supply. The Pope is nowhere in sight. We buy a bag of chick starter, a heat lamp, a clip-on thermometer, a chick-watering pan, and a chick-feed trough. Grand total, $46.

So much for "free" eggs and meat. Are chicken accessories tax-deductible? I make a mental note to check. The money for all this came from my tax-refund check—a godsend that arrived a few days ago in the mail.

Behind the store by the Dumpster I find a big empty cardboard box with the words "Farm Play Set" printed on the side. I rip the top flaps off as cleanly as I can and shove it into the back of the van.

Back home, we go out to the barn together and assemble a chicken condo that would make even Chicken Little feel secure. Our work finally done, we kneel down in silence, place our hands in our laps, and watch as the chicks get their bearings.

They hop around, peck at their food, peck at the newspaper, peck each other and peck the cardboard. Their seed-sized hearts are beating fast, and the only sound is their cheeping.

The barn is dimly lit and I can feel the May chill sneaking up under the back of my sweater. Warmth and light radiate from the heat lamp. The glow reflects on Will's face, and with his freckles, his blond hair, his oversize hooded sweatshirt, he looks like a modern-day cherub.

"Look, Mom," he whispers. "Safe and sound."

For the chaos he accidentally wrought down upon the meadow voles, he is now redeemed. And in this moment, in the filtered light, with the hay dust glistening, he has grown wings.

In the coming days, our baby chicks grow quickly and our financial reckoning closes in. The green minivan is Mr. Wonderful's now and I'm down to just Cookie for transportation, so the four of us can't go anywhere together—at least not safely or legally. Even more worrisome, though, is the issue of our home, our land, our farm, and the mortgage refinance.

"We have a glitch," the loan broker tells me.

No woman wants to hear her mortgage broker tell her that. Certainly not me. And certainly not after everything I've been through with my sons already. We've survived for nearly a year on squash, pilfered firewood, purple climbing rope, *Finding Utopia*, and spiritual longing. Lady, I'd like to tell her, we are pretty sick of glitches.

At the divorce hearing in March, the judge allotted me ninety days to find a bank willing to refinance the farmhouse in my name only. I've asked every bank in town for a loan, and their universal answer is a resounding, echoing "No, ma'am."

More than half of my ninety days are past, and so the odds of me being able to make the payments on this place wouldn't tempt the most desperate compulsive gambler.

Even though Mr. Wonderful has paid his child support on time every single month, and even though I am still getting a *Utopia* paycheck, and even though I'm paying most of our bills, I'm still paying them late. Every month it seems that our moon wanes a little more and we are getting farther and farther behind.

So despite the fact that their rates are a lot higher, I've begun negotiating with the finance company that holds the current mortgage on the Big Valley—the company that approved the mortgage application when I was married. And they're the ones who have informed me of said "glitch." Even though I've pitched them a perfectly good financing idea that requires nothing more complicated than a common office supply: Wite-Out.

Can't the underwriter just dip the magic brush into the little bottle of liquid and paint over Mr. Wonderful's name? Um, no, Rebecca, I'm afraid they really can't.

"It's your credit rating," the mortgage broker says glumly,

as if giving me a medical diagnosis. "It came back 'Seriously Delinquent.'"

In the past month I've spent more than a hundred dollars on chickens and their accessories, so that we can have free eggs instead of paying a dollar fifty a dozen for them. I've spent that much again on seeds to plant in soil that I might not even own in a few months. I'm still in debt for the well to water these seeds that will be planted in that same tenuous soil. These are examples of the kind of high-grade financial genius that I am.

But I do know how to manipulate people sometimes, and this just happens to be one of those times.

"I thought you said you could get *anyone* a mortgage," I taunt.

"Well," the broker says, giving me a big sigh, "if you could come up with some decent collateral, something easily liquidated, I could resubmit."

Right, I think. *Hold the line and give me just one sec and I'll pull that stuff right out of my ass.*

"I'll see what I can do," I tell her.

"Super!" she sings back and clicks off the line.

We are not, as Will just observed about our new baby chicks, safe and sound. Not even close.

I've done everything I can think of to bring in extra money. I've sold the pasture fencing and the wood and hardware from the horse stalls and even the few remaining bales of hay that were still stacked in the barn. I've sold some furniture I was storing in the garage. My parents are buying a new minivan and have offered to give me their old one to replace the one I just lost in the divorce. I accept it with relief and gratitude, and then sell off my truck, Cookie, too. All this brings in a few thousand dollars and helps catch me up on my bills, but it's not enough to be considered any kind of collateral.

I'm speeding through my ninety days now hell-bent-for-leather. Time's a runaway horse and I'm strapped on.

Funny thing, but it's actually easier to plan a chicken coop than it is to find decent mortgage collateral, which is maybe why I spend the next week in chicken-related denial. If I really accepted the possibility that we could lose the farm, I wouldn't be adding to the population of beings who live here.

But I cannot and will not accept that possibility. And so I plan a permanent home for the chickens instead, as if this will somehow make the Big Valley our permanent home, too.

Plus, the chicks don't care about my credit rating and just continue to grow regardless. They are quickly outgrowing their cardboard condo and within ten days of their arrival, we can even tell the meat chickens from the egg chickens. The egg chickens are still small and cute. Still lemon yellow, though they are bigger now and their tiny wing feathers are starting to grow. The meat chickens have turned a dirty white, are beefed up, and they lumber around the box like fat children. They dwarf the egg chickens and crowd the food trough. They are bullies.

"That one looks like this one kid in my class," Will says, pointing at a big white chick that is cocking its head and staring us in the eye.

In the next two weeks, the meat chickens triple in size and the egg chickens grow a little bit, too. We move them first into a blue plastic kiddie pool the boys have outgrown, and then into an empty refrigerator box I find next to the recycling station at the township dump.

Then, we name them.

The meat chickens we just call "the Meats," because they are not individual beings, they are a pack. Plus, the plan is to eat them, and after our experience with Rocky, naming them doesn't seem right.

But the egg chickens are more like separate beings, we aren't going to eat them, we'll hopefully have them for a long time, perhaps several years, and they deserve names. There are Alice, Cher (tall and the longest-legged), Mrs. Donahue (named after my long-ago kindergarten teacher), Fluffy, Clucker, Pink Ranger (of Power Ranger fame), Missy, Prissy, Gladys, and Star.

For ease of care and so it can be seen from the house, the coop will be built in a corner of the vegetable garden. We are three miles south of the east arm of Grand Traverse Bay, and without regular enrichments our soil is still like beach sand, and so I'm also thinking free fertilizer. Chicken manure is the richest poop of all, better in nutrients than dairy cow, horse, steer, rabbit, or sheep doo. It's so rich that it has to be composted first or it will actually burn your vegetable plants. I want me some of that.

On a windy and cold day in late May, Luke and I stand side by side on the rise next to the driveway and look down at the garden. We will need to build a shelter for the chickens to roost in at night and during bad weather, nesting boxes for them to lay their eggs in, easy access to the nesting boxes so we can collect the eggs, and a fenced-in yard for exercise. The exercise yard will have to have a roof of chicken wire to keep out hawks yet be tall enough for us to walk inside of and clean.

Luke sets down his toolbox and stares silently at the building site. He is almost as tall as I am now and, of my three sons, is the one that people are most likely to say looks like me. He has long fingers, and there are gold flecks in his green eyes. He is wearing a Metallica T-shirt under his camouflage jacket. His light-brown curls show below his black knit cap. He is architect, builder, boy.

"Got any ideas?" I ask.

"I'm thinking," he says, without looking at me.

A minute later he suggests calling into use an old wooden playhouse he and his brothers have long since abandoned. It's heavy, it's an eyesore, and it's stuck back at the edge of the woods. But it is the right size and has another obvious advantage—it's already built. I like the idea, and the job changes from one of building to one of moving. He knows the drill.

"I'll get some kids," he says.

Luke has always been good at getting kids here to help us with big jobs like this. Quite an accomplishment, considering how far we live outside of town, with no neighbors, sidewalks, or bike paths. But somehow, he still gets them here.

Kids arrive on their bikes, on foot, and even get dropped off by their busy parents in their SUVs. One friend of Luke's has a flock of chickens at his house that range free, and he doesn't understand why we are building a coop but comes by to help out anyway. Maybe it's the curiosity factor.

Then Owen catches wind of what we're up to, gets on the phone, and Aberration shows up to help, too. The project, the band members say with utter seriousness, has songwriting potential, and I can't help it, I think "Armageddon Chicken" has a nice ring to it. Perhaps that's just my desperation talking.

These kids do not ask to be paid for their labor, which I couldn't do anyway, but only expect macaroni and cheese from a box, homemade cookies, cheese quesadillas, and, depending on the season, Kool-Aid or hot chocolate, plus plenty of admiration, which I do have.

The kids and the rock band arrive and we gather at the play-house. There is a lot of pushing and lifting and groaning, but the playhouse is just too heavy to move.

"It's built too well," I say. "The wood is too heavy."

Luke not only looks a little like me, he has my stubbornness. Tell him something can't be done and he has an irresistible urge to floor his internal accelerator. But where I tend to bulldoze, he problem-solves.

"We could roll it," he says, "like a ginormous snowball."

And that is what we do. We tip the four-by-seven-foot wood playhouse on its side and roll it out of the woods, up a little hill, around the barn, and down another hill toward the edge of the garden. Just exactly like a ginormous snowball.

There is something silly about a small building rolling down a hill on its side. And I can't help it, this image reminds me of my own ridiculous effort over the past several weeks to obtain a mort-gage. You wouldn't think so, but a weather-beaten, waterlogged wooden playhouse somersaulting, picking up speed, and tossing off paint chips and loose boards on the way down does call to mind principal and interest.

Once it's at the proper location, though, we right the play-house, shove it back and forth until the door faces the garden, and cheer. The younger boys bend one knee and shove their fists in the air like the soldiers of Iwo Jima. Will's best friend, Joey, puts his cupped hand to his mouth and makes a bugling sound.

Thank God for boys, I say to myself. *Thank God for comic relief.*

"Hot chocolate and cookies for the coop brigade!" I say out loud.

While they're snacking in the kitchen, I come back outside and take another look at the thing. It is crooked, the door is broken off, and it's two and a half feet out from the garden shed. It would look better and be a more efficient use of space if the two buildings were in line with each other. Two feet is too small a distance for another roll, but too far to push the heavy thing.

"Got any ideas?" Luke asks, chewing on a cookie.

"I'm thinking," I say.

After a minute, I walk to my new used minivan, start it up, drive it off our paved driveway, over the grass, and down the hill toward the garden, until the rubber bumper just touches the side of the playhouse. I gently press on the gas pedal and the playhouse and the minivan and I move forward. I keep this up until the two buildings are even, then I drive the minivan back and park it in its spot in the driveway.

When I get out, Luke is grinning at me. I go fetch the roll of chicken wire and he holds up his staple gun in salute. We study what is no longer an abandoned playhouse but, in our minds, a respectable coop.

"Not bad lodging," he says, "if you're a chicken."

Over the next several days we finish the coop, move the chickens in, and I turn my attention from animals to plants. It's time to plot out the garden beds, and I sort seeds like the Big Valley is already ours. Growing a garden is a sign of permanence. Of faith.

What's the point of planting at all if we're just going to lose the place? There isn't one. Even though planting makes me feel grounded to this spot, to my land, to my home; even I know that it isn't an assurance of anything.

The spinach, lettuce, and radishes are in, but I'm running late with the sweet corn and the tomatoes. These tender-stalked heavy feeders each need a long season to mature—seventy to ninety days for the corn and about fifty to sixty-five days for the tomatoes if you plant seedlings instead of seeds—and time's a-wasting.

The Big Valley is located in the USDA's Hardiness Zone 5, which means it doesn't usually get colder than twenty degrees below zero in the winter. It also means that the last day that gardeners here can expect a frost is June 9, and the first day we need to start worrying about frost again is September 17. In between is time to make hay—and tomatoes, broccoli, corn, lettuce, spinach, and all the rest if we want to eat this winter.

Our official growing season is approximately one hundred days long, but I've got to extend it if I want to grow enough food to sustain us. Where will we be in one hundred days? Here, eating our own sweet corn and our own chickens, if I have anything to say about it.

By mid-May, then, the corn seeds should be soaked, planted, and covered over with a tarp to protect them from the crows until they germinate. The tomato seedlings should be in the ground now, their roots turned out at a right angle to stimulate good growth and a big root system. And each plant should be buried up to its neck in compost and crushed eggshells.

I use ingenious little individual greenhouses called Wall O' Water to extend our growing season. These are a simple invention, just bands of vinyl tubes you fill with tap water and shape in a cone around tender seedlings like tomato, eggplant, pepper, and herbs. They soak up the warmth of the sun during the day and keep the plants from freezing at night. Time it right and even on the cold edge of Zone 5, you can have ripe tomatoes by the end of July or the beginning of August.

That's always been my goal—tomatoes by July 31. Some years I make it and some years I don't, but like most deadlines, in order to have a chance of meeting this one you have to calculate backwards. And my seedlings should have been hardened off and planted, like, yesterday.

"Making the earth say beans instead of grass—this was my daily work," writes Thoreau in *Walden*.

By the end of May, my daily work should have been making the garden say spaghetti sauce and salsa. Making it say corn fresh from the cob stuck in my sons' teeth at dinner, canning jars hot-packed with dilly beans and cucumber pickles.

But this week I've been busy with writing assignments and filling out mortgage paperwork and I'm behind schedule, and instead of saying beans, the 60-by-140-foot patch of compost-and-horse-manure-enriched dirt where I am supposed to be growing our breakfast, lunch, and dinner is saying, "Rototill me."

And it's when my mind has gone slack and is focused on worms that I figure out how to deal with the mortgage company. The day is warm and steam rises off the soil as I walk behind a borrowed garden tiller. Dead leaves, brown pine needles, compost from our compost pile, calcified horse turds from Major and Pepper, food scraps, my own sweat, and the soy-ink newspapers I used as pathways last season all grind in. I watch my soil turn from a dusty and overwintered gray to a lovely black, rich and moist as devil's food cake.

Tilling this large plot makes planting easier, but there is a downside to it: you destroy the worm casts—tunnels of worm poo that make terrific fertilizer and also aerate the soil so it holds water better—and cut up many of the helpful worms that made them. Because of this, I only till every third year. This is a tilling year, and worms are going to suffer for it. Most of them will grow into full worms again, but some will die, and as I watch pieces of worms come to the surface I have my first helpful thought.

Like the worms, this land was also once in pieces too—on paper, anyway.

The house sits on a two-and-a-half-acre piece, and the pasture and the woods were once divided into two additional two-acre pieces. I had all three parcels resurveyed into a single one again when we built the barn, because in order to keep horses in our township, there's a five-acre minimum lot size.

But the horses are gone. That girlhood dream is over, and I can't bear the thought of ever having horses here again. So it's possible that I could have the lots resurveyed, replotted back into three separate parcels, improving my on-paper finances. The current mortgage was written back when the property was in three pieces and it was written only on the farmhouse's parcel. I own the other two vacant parcels outright. They are unmortgaged real estate. And it's possible that I could get approved for a new mortgage just by resurveying my property and using the vacant land as collateral.

I leave the tiller parked in the middle of the garden, surrounded by writhing worms glinting in the sun. My sprint leaves big footprints in the new soil, headed straight for the house. Inside, I go right to my file cabinet and dig out the old survey. I was right. It shows my farmhouse and my six and one-half acres divided as three separate parcels. At the bottom is the surveyor's name and telephone number.

Could it really be this easy? Just make a phone call to the surveyor, ask him to resurvey my property, pass the information on to my broker, and get approved for a new mortgage?

Like most questions in my life now, the answer turns out to be yes and no. Yes, it is almost that easy to resurvey the property—for a fee, of course—and yes, once my adjacent land is resurveyed it will be free of debt and can be used as collateral on the application. But no, the mortgage broker says, it's not enough collateral on its own to get the application approved. I'm still going to need something else too, something liquid and real that can be turned into quick cash, not something manipulated out of thin air with survey tape and a compass.

While digging through the file cabinet looking for the land survey, my fingers walked over another file folder, marked "Boys' Stock." It's been down here all along, but it never occurred to me to use it as collateral. That's because this stock doesn't belong to me, it belongs to my sons.

A note inside the file, in the shaky handwriting of my ninety-six-year-old grandpa, reads: "I would hope that this fund would be used for education. If not, down payment on property for these kids when they grow up. But I won't be here so you will need to make the decision." Signed "GP," for Grandpa.

My parents would cringe if they knew I was even thinking these thoughts. They are both educators. Nothing in life is more important to them than education. But they don't know everything. And keeping the farm isn't just for me, I rationalize; it's for my sons, too. They'll only lose their college money if I default. Which I won't. Will. Not.

And so with sixteen days to spare, my mortgage application is approved. By sheer force of will, or desperation, or manipulation, or all three, I am approved for a mortgage on the Big Valley. And that's not nothing.

· · ·

The good-bye that puts an ache in my chest so deep it feels almost ancestral begins with, of all things, a picnic. Believe me, I've tried to think of something else—*anything* else. But there's no getting around it.

It's the last Saturday in May, three days after I've signed the new mortgage, and it's sunny outside. A little chilly, a little windy, but tomorrow a thunderstorm is predicted, and so if I'm going to do this at all, it has to be today. And I have to do it.

All three boys are in the garden, subjected to their daily weeding torture. The spinach, lettuce, beets, and radishes are up, the onion sets are in, and so is the sweet corn.

I've got forty-five tomato seedlings on a rack on the porch, just beginning to accept the idea of going into the ground, and forty-five boy-dug holes to put them in when they do. That will probably happen tomorrow, Sunday, after the storm comes through.

We haven't been to church in a month and there won't be time to go this week, either. And, truth be told, I don't miss it. There's too much work to do here this time of year, and the boys and I need all seven days to complete it. A day of rest is out of the question. We barely have time for this lunch break, but it isn't optional.

"Picnic lunch time!" I holler.

The boys lift their heads from their rakes, and from their dirty fingernails, and from the evil dead nettle, pokeweed, and curly dock that have become their enemy. They see me walking out the door, carrying a blanket and a Thermos of lemonade.

"Picnics are for girls," Luke says.

"So are cookies!" I yell back, holding up four bulging brown lunch sacks. At the sight of actual food, they put down their tools, turn on the pump, wash their hands, and follow me away from the garden, around the edge of the pasture, and toward a flat place in the grass on the back lot.

Over my shoulder I see them twenty paces behind me, boys in various stages of becoming men, stuck following a woman, and I wonder how much longer this will last. They are sixteen, thirteen, and nine now. Soon they are not going to want to follow me at all anymore, especially not Owen.

I spread the blanket out on the grass under a group of doomed elm saplings, rooted here by chance from seeds released to the wind by their slowly dying ancestor, the big tree near the house shriveled by disease and parasitic beetles. These saplings show signs of the same malady, and will probably have the energy to leaf out only one or two more summers. Perhaps a bulldozer will just take them quick.

I pour cups of lemonade while the boys unfold the wax paper on their sandwiches—Swiss cheese and hummus for Owen, the vegetarian; turkey, peanut butter, pickles, and lettuce for Luke, the epicurean adventurer; and the usual for Will, crunchy peanut butter and our homemade jam.

We chew and discuss the breaking news of the morning—the broad-winged hawk that has been circling the chicken coop again; the poisonous northern black widow spider they found in its web on a fence post, captured in a screen-sided bug cage, then drowned in a bucket; their own weeding prowess.

"The ragweed sees me coming and starts shaking in its roots!" Luke says, laughing at his own pun.

When we're almost finished with our sandwiches and apples, I bring out the homemade snickerdoodles I've promised them. It's weak, I know, thinking cinnamon sugar cookies can offset what

I'm about to tell them, but when it comes right down to it, that's what I've got.

"I have some sad news," I tell them.

All chewing stops. What, they must be wondering, is she going to lay on us now? In the past eleven months I have used this line to announce my divorce from their father, to break the news of Major's death, to tell them I sold Pepper, to tell them Rocky's time was up, and even to ease into my admission that they were on the free-lunch list at school. After getting approved for the mortgage, it took me about a day to realize it was a mortgage I could afford only on paper. I'm going to go broke without a big infusion of cash. News I can't hide from my sons. I'm not getting any better at ripping off the Band-Aid, though.

"We've got to sell the land. It's the only way we can afford to keep the house."

"What land?" Luke asks, his mouth full of sandwich. His tone suggests we own large tracts in exotic places far, far away that he's never contemplated or seen. I wish.

"This land," I say. "The land you're sitting on."

Owen just shakes his head, but Will gets that frown his forehead produces when our shifting life doesn't yet make sense to him.

"This isn't *land*," he says, as if my announcement were the most foolish thing he's ever heard. "This is our *yard*."

The survey simply calls this square of dirt "Parcel A," and its neighbor "Parcel B." The dimensions and legal description have been notarized, so they must be spot-on. Yet that document can't begin to describe what this land means to me. To us.

Because where on that piece of paper does it record Will and me walking hand in hand on a bug safari, him sad because his brothers left him every day to go to school? Where is the route all four of us would take on moonlit walks in the summertime, turning off the flashlight, lying on our backs in the field, and looking up at all creation? And there are no X's for Luke's bow-and-arrow targets, or for the boys' tree forts, or Owen's bike trails. Nothing identifies our award-winning zucchini patch, either.

Major's last stand will not go down into this record, either, I guess.

And all of these things, these memories, are what I'm really selling, not just a couple acres of dirt.

But there are no real secrets in families, and so I have to tell them this. And so I bottom-line them.

"Monday a For Sale sign is going up," I manage to choke out.

I see my own face then reflected back at me in their navy, hazel-green, and blue eyes. And I see that I've aged. I am a hundred years older and a hundred winters wearier now, when our six and a half acres are about to become four, than I was last summer, when the five of us became four.

I think of those displaced meadow voles and Will's pronouncement that people wreck everything, and I have never felt so defeated. Not when I sat in the courtroom, not when I drove my children around collecting firewood, not even when I had the flu.

A year ago, selling even a blade of grass off Big Valley land was unthinkable. But every moon's relentless shine since then has brought me, heels dragging, nearer and nearer to casting this crescent-shaped shadow over the four of us. And now, this afternoon, gripped in my very own hand, if it isn't the devil's scythe—and I've even got it raised up, poised to swing.

12

June 2006

DEVIL'S MOON

The wind was a torrent of darkness among the gusty trees.
The moon was a ghostly galleon tossed upon cloudy seas.
The road was a ribbon of moonlight over the purple moor,
And the highwayman came riding—
Riding—riding—
The highwayman came riding, up to the old inn-door.

—ALFRED NOYES, "The Highwayman"

It's the afternoon of the day my land is listed for sale, my realtor says her line is ringing steady, and although the sky is clear, I feel the buzzards kettling.

Most of these scavengers just peck my realtor's brain over the phone for information on the terms I'm offering (cash only) and any special selling points of the property (water view), but a particularly aggressive buyer has the gall to swoop in personally.

I am alerted to his presence when I am inside to get a drink of water and hear large boots walking up my front steps. I can count on less than one hand the men who have a legitimate reason to frequent the Big Valley: Mr. Wonderful, here to pick up or drop off the boys; the mailman, if I've received a package of seeds, tubers, or rootstock too large to fit in my mailbox; or the well driller, here to nudge me for a payment.

Occasionally Pete checks in to see if the remodel is back on (it's not), and sometimes stays to talk awhile even though the snow is more than two months gone. I'm beginning to think he wants my company. And he does wear work boots, but I know the sound of them now, and the squeaky ones I just heard are not his.

Sneaking a look out the window, I see that this visitor is tall and ravenlike, clad in biker gear from his do-rag to his leather pants, and is sporting a limp little mustache. He runs a gloved finger over the back of one of my lavender metal chairs, then bends down and sniffs a flowerpot full of pink and green coleus. This is a brightly variegated tropical plant grown for its decorative foliage and not its flowers, which are negligible and have no smell.

So *this* is who I'm sacrificing my land to? Please, no.

But the visitor continues to sniff away for a few more useless seconds, then stands up straight as a pitchfork, takes off his gloves with a couple of quick jerks, holds them with his right hand, and slaps them against the palm of his left. This is a man not used to being kept waiting.

"When the devil is knocking on your door," my grandma Link would say, "just yell, 'Hey, Jesus, would you mind getting that for me?'"

I wish she were here. I wish I didn't have to sell my land. But Grandma Link is five years gone, wishes aren't going to get me anywhere, and I'm going to have to handle this myself, which along with being necessary is also supremely annoying. I have another hour before the boys get home from school, prime work time, and I wanted to use it weeding the sweet corn, which is just starting to ear up, and re-outfitting the scarecrow, not to chasing off this joker.

So go ahead and stop me then if you've heard this one: a perfectly good day, interrupted by an unwelcome man. And it occurs to me that there have been more than just a few of these types intruding on me over the past year, and always at the very worst time, like a record scratch just when the song was getting to my favorite part. Can't life just leave me alone for a little while?

"Helloooo?" my visitor calls through the screen door, right on cue. "I'm looking for the owner of that lovely lot for sale."

I pull my face back from my spying window, take a breath, grit my teeth, and approach my front door.

"You're lookin' at her," I say to him, with all the hospitality of a picker bush.

I've accepted the fact that I have to sell the land to keep our farmhouse. Barely. The For Sale sign is up and the listing is published. But that doesn't mean I have to get friendly with whichever vulture is going to be pecking the flesh from my bones. That's the realtor's job. That's what I'll be paying a commission for.

"Oh, well! Hello, then!" he says, ignoring my vibe. "My mother is in assisted living around the corner and I'm looking to move somewhere's around here. I love your purple chairs, by the way. This whole place, all your flowers, it's just darling!"

This place *is* just darling, I think. This place rocks the living daylights out of darling. And I try to keep my hackles up just like this,

I really do, but I can feel my demeanor change, just a little. Compliment the farm the boys and I have worked so hard for and I'll probably give you arterial blood, not to mention the time of day.

"Why don't we talk outside," I say, resigned now to this interruption. "Grab a seat. Would you like a glass of ice tea?"

He would. I don't have any instant, and I'll have to make it from scratch out of tea bags, boiling water, and ice cubes, but it's hot and humid outside, and this man's odd, squeaky voice and chipper manner have gotten the best of me, even if I suspect both traits might be fake.

I watch the water boil on the stove and think, *Really? This is the guy? This is my new neighbor?* I actually hadn't given any thought to who it was going to be until now. None.

When a person loses a limb, I'm pretty sure they don't try to imagine it living an active new life attached to someone else's body. Which is why I hadn't given any thought to who would be buying my land, I just considered it about to be amputated. Even if I had taken the time to think about it, this is definitely *not* who I would have conjured.

But when you are desperate, you don't get to choose your patron. Nope, when you are as desperate for money as I am, you pretty much just get what you get.

In fifteen minutes over sweaty glasses of weak tea this potential buyer knows a tiny bit of my story and I know a lot of his. This high-voiced biker with the little mustache is newly single and the only one of his four siblings who lives close enough to their frail mother to look after her affairs. He has a double-wide (*a trailer?*) and can afford to finance (*finance?*) the land purchase because he has income from an unnamed source. Buried gold bullion? Military pension? I don't ask—not because it's impolite but because it isn't going to matter.

He rambles on, but the iron gate in my brain that swung open a crack at the words "just darling" locks shut now. I am going to have to accept that there is still a good life for the boys and me here on the Big Valley after our woods and pasture are cut off and owned by someone else. But it isn't going to be *this* someone else. He's dropped two words into the conversation that just aren't going to fly—"finance" and "double-wide"—and now I know why he came to see me directly instead of calling my realtor like any reputable buyer would do. He's here for the hornswoggle.

My listing specifically states no land contracts and no mobile homes, and I know even with those restrictions there's been a lot of interest in the listing already. Meaning, I am desperate, but I still don't have to take the first offer that comes along.

This guy doesn't want to build a house, he wants to move a trailer here, then trickle a little money my way every month for the privilege. After the well and the mortgage debacles, I know everything I want to know about financing. Being on the other end of debt, the collection end, might not be anything I'm accustomed to, but it's not anything I can afford, either.

This visit, then, is just what I thought it was before the tea and hospitality—another day interrupted by another unwelcome man. I ponder this and a full cast of his ilk saunters through my mind. This man in black who has shown up uninvited might as well be Edgar, the koi-killing bird; Shark, the Goodwill inmate; SAVED, the carnival thief; Count Olaf, the real-estate appraiser; Beard, the court's social worker; or, yes, even Mr. Wonderful, the ex-husband.

"The deal is for cash only," I tell him. "And no trailers."

At my bluntness, his hand goes straight to his Adam's apple.

"I do *not* have a trailer," he says, aghast. "I live in a 1998 manufactured home that meets or exceeds all your township's zoning regulations. I already checked."

"Well, the answer's still no," I say. "I'm not selling to you. I'm sorry."

My visitor puts down his glass of tea and quickly stands. He pulls out his wallet, takes out a business card, and snaps it down on the table.

"In case you change your mind," he says.

Then he smooths his coat, strides toward the porch steps, starts down, changes his mind, and spins around to face me one last time.

"See *that!*" he says, pointing at a big rock that Will hand-painted to look like a ladybug, complete with glued-on wiggly eyes. "It's *tacky!*"

I acknowledge his exit with a cheerful wave.

June is actually one of the prettiest months on the Big Valley. The lawn is a new green, the early-summer flowers are starting to bloom, and the garden is alive with all the colors and textures of vegetables just beginning to grow. The cherry trees still have a few blossoms left, and the poppies in the perennial border are just past their peak. So at the slightest breeze, giant orange petals float through the air. The waterfall in the koi pond sparkles, and my wraparound porch is decorated with hanging baskets of purple petunias, blooming planters of coleus, and vintage knick-knacks.

But when I steel my unflinching eye there are a few landmarks beyond rock art that just might, in someone else's world, be considered "tacky." But so what? So what if there is a dead chest freezer sitting at the edge of my driveway, waiting to be hauled to the dump. So what if there is a tent the boys set up in the yard for a sleepover last month. So what if the grass is long and there sits my broken lawn mower.

In a perfect world, the freezer would be gone, the lawn would be mowed, and the tent would be packed away. But in a perfect world, I wouldn't be selling my land.

I've still got a half hour to finish the tasks at hand, the sweet-corn weeding and the scarecrow outfitting, and I'm thankful that the boys aren't home from school yet. That at least Will didn't have to hear the insult that man leveled down upon his rock art. And on a whim, I take a look at the business card he left behind, read the name, and grin. If the man who comes to buy your land is named Foxworthy, you might be a redneck.

I hum while I weed the sweet corn, then rummage through the back of my closet for some new clothes for the scarecrow. The crows have gotten wise to his straw-stuffed jeans and faded flannel shirt, and he's way overdue for a new look. I find a long flowered skirt that I'll never wear again and a Hawaiian shirt Mr. Wonderful left behind. A light breeze blows, poppy petals float by, the scarecrow's skirt ripples, and it's time for the boys to get home from school.

I hear them pound up the front steps then, and I call hello and wave to them from the garden before they run into the house for an after-school snack. They wave back, then bang through the screen door.

All is right with our world, again. We've been interrupted before, and we'll no doubt be interrupted again. We've dealt with thieves, predators, judges, and drillers, and there will probably be other adversaries in our future. And I know we are going to have to sell part of our land, and soon, too, but just look at everything we've held on to.

The boys inside, I throw the prospective buyer's calling card in the trash.

A week later I have a purchase agreement for my land, and it's not with Mr. Foxworthy.

The new buyer has a blueprint for a two-story house back in my woods of Christmas trees with a long driveway stretching straight through Major's pasture and out to the road. As I consider the plan on paper, my empty barn looks like a big red hand I can keep over my eyes so that after the buyer's new house is built, I won't even have to see it. A blessing, I suppose, if there is one to be found in this transaction, and I sign on the dotted line.

I get on the phone to my creditors and give them the good news. I owe property taxes, soccer fees for Will, I haven't paid the gas bill since the end of winter and there's an impending shutoff. Owen and Luke both won partial scholarships to music camp, and the remainder of their tuition is looming. The tires on the silver minivan were solid when my parents gave it to me, but with our hard use are now bald as Kojak. There's credit-card debt, the well-repair bill, and I still owe my parents the money they loaned me almost a year ago for my divorce attorney.

I add up all these trespasses. They are significant, but as soon as I close on the land sale, I'll be back to even with enough left over to make up a respectable savings account. And on June 28, just two days before my first payment is due on the new mortgage, I walk out of Mid-American Title Company with a big check. I sit in my minivan and put the check on the dashboard and just stare at it for a few minutes.

I just sold land that, as far as I know, has never been built on before. Not in the whole history of time. Land that was wild, land that was carved by glaciers, then inhabited by the ancients, then cultivated, then grazed by dairy cows, then grazed by Major and Pepper, then produced prizewinning zucchini, then was sacrificed.

By me.

I am, in this long ownership chain, quite literally the weakest Link. And yet, when it comes to giving my sons a home, I am tough enough.

Breaking my land apart and selling part of it off will save us. I'm sacrificing the dream of a real farm, the dream of horses, a pasture, and a big pine woods, for the reality of what my family of four really is now: solvent. My rural heart is broken, but for once my bank account is not. And my sons' college accounts are safe.

I blow my nose on a dried-up wet nap I find in my new used minivan's glove box, make out a deposit ticket, and say, *Thank you.*

It comes out like a prayer, but a prayer to whom, I'm still not sure.

We've stopped going to church, and instead I've made it a point every day, sometimes several times a day, to slow down. To think. To be present. And I've even tried to pass on this reverence for our lives, in small ways at least, to my sons.

Sitting here in my minivan, losing something I'm so very attached to, I know all my spiritual questions remain, but instead of being rankled by this I have a sudden but comforting thought: Maybe this spiritual questioning isn't really confusion, after all.

Maybe it's inquiry. Maybe it's curiosity. And maybe it's not even a problem to solve, but just a permanent part of my character.

"Do we need to make a special effort to enjoy the beauty of the blue sky?" asks Thich Nhat Hanh. "No, we just enjoy it."

I can live with that.

My thank-you prayer echoes, and I feel my world fill up with gratitude. I am aware of my surroundings, and my immediate blessings are enormous. All this time I've been so busy asking for things, I haven't even considered what you're supposed to do when you receive them.

Please let the boys sleep through Major's ugly death. *Please* help me survive this flu. *Please* let me go on a date with Pete. *Please* let us keep the Big Valley. *Please.*

All of those prayers have been answered. And even though I have to let part of my land go, I've been able to keep so much more, and it's finally occurring to me to say thank you for the privilege of our rural lives.

Faith, whether it's in Jesus, or a church, or the power of the human mind to connect, isn't ever going to be a meaningful force in my life if it's always one-sided. Faith, connection, spirituality—none of it means very much if it's always with the please, please, please, but never a single thank-you.

"What are you doing here?" Will asked when I picked him up from school the day our baby chicks arrived. Answering that question will take more than a month, more than a year, more than twelve full moons, it will take a lifetime. And it will start with *"Thank you."*

. . .

It's the weekend some time in the future; the boys are at their father's again and I am home alone. I've tuned the television to our public-access station, hoping to catch the broadcast of a township meeting. Municipal water lines are about to be installed along my road and I want to know the details, especially since I finally own this place. But instead of talking heads around a conference table, there on the TV is my green minivan. The one Mr. Wonderful scored in our divorce.

And it is on fire.

Smoke funnels out of the side door and flames lick the undercarriage. An off-camera narrator is explaining that firefighters train in controlled burns like this one for several hours each year in order to retain their certification. Sometimes they gut old house trailers and light them on fire; sometimes they ignite wooden burn towers built specifically for the purpose, and sometimes they light junk cars like this one.

Wait just a flaming minute, I think. *Junk?*

I crouch close to my TV, stare at the screen, and tell myself that this green Ford Windstar with the jagged line of rust along the driver's door, the American flag suction-cupped to an inside window, and the "I'd Rather Be Reading Jane Austen" bumper sticker couldn't possibly belong to any other family.

I can accept losing the van to Mr. Wonderful if he really needs it to transport our sons to their school activities and orchestra concerts and drive them back and forth to friends' houses on the weekends when they are with him. I can face losing this comfortable vehicle and accepting the newer one from my parents with relief and gratitude if it means that my sons won't have to ride in his work van.

But I'm going to have a hard time with losing it if he took it away from me just so that he could burn it down.

"Because each divorce is unique," the SMILE handbook advises, "divorcing couples should consult psychological services, support groups, conflict and mediation agencies, and books or articles relating to divorce."

My divorce must be *really* unique, because it has involved a work-release inmate, a social worker, lawyers, judges, bill collectors, bankers, preachers, real-estate agents, a Christian well driller, and a tower of library books about Buddhism. I can add firefighters-in-training to that list now, too, I guess.

The firefighters unroll a huge wheel of hose, but this is not the kind of water line I turned on the TV to see, and there isn't enough of it in the whole world to cool me off right now. Whatever small glow of compassion and acceptance I've fanned in my heart hardens again like charcoal.

"Here come the jaws of life!" the off-camera narrator announces, as hydraulic pincers crack open the side of my old van like fangs through a soft-boiled egg. It feels like my own ribs are being spread apart.

This is only a car, I tell myself. Just a thing, an object with no soul or feelings, a hunk of inanimate steel, plastic, wires, and rubber. But that doesn't make me feel any better.

Because it was also once a symbol to me of motherhood, a symbol of having children to ferry around safely. It once carried my sons and me wherever we needed to go, along with firewood and baby chicks, hay bales and tomato seedlings, guitar amplifiers and library books. Now it's just a container for everything I've lost.

And it is burning to the ground.

"All things, O priests, are on fire," Siddhartha said, before he became the Buddha. "The eye is on fire; forms are on fire; eye-consciousness is on fire; impressions received by the eye are on fire."

Is this my shot at enlightenment? Somehow I doubt it, and I want to shut my eyes to it but I'm riveted. A dummy in the front seat and a smaller dummy in the backseat are cut free from their seat belts and dragged to safety before smoke and flames engulf the green van entirely. A smiling but sooty firefighter is interviewed, the program ends, and I turn the television off.

"Parents should not jump to conclusions before getting all the information," advises my SMILE handbook. "A parent should not ask children what goes on in the other parent's home. This is a violation of children's trust."

Whatever.

"What's going on with the green van?" I ask Luke the second I get him alone.

He and his brothers walked over from across the road this afternoon instead of being dropped off in the van by Mr. Wonderful, providing me with an innocent enough reason for asking about it. Owen reads me like a billboard, and Will isn't always aware of events beyond his nine-year-old world, so when I am at my worst and use one of my sons for my own devices, it is easygoing Luke I violate.

"Oh yeah, so this is pretty cool," he tells me, eyes sparkling. "The transmission broke, and dad said it would cost too much to fix it, so he donated it to the fire department. They burned it. It was awesome."

Because of his father's good-hearted charity, Luke explains

proudly, if a mom and her kids are ever trapped inside a burning minivan, our local firefighters will all know exactly how to save their lives.

And that's when the hottest, still-glowing embers of bitterness smoldering in my heart go out, just like that.

13

July 2006

MAN IN THE MOON

No one, including me, especially anymore believes
till death do us part,
but I can see what I would miss in leaving—
the way her ankles go into the work boots
as she stands upon the ice chest;
the problem scrunched into her forehead;
the little kissable mouth
with the nail in it.

—TONY HOAGLAND, "Windchime"

The Big Valley looks different to me now. Like a photograph carefully edited, the definition and color-saturation levels cranked up as far as they will go. It's ours now, *ours!*, and the frantic work that has been my refuge over the past year is my daily security now. Today, this work is even a joy, and there's a sense of purpose to our labor that I haven't felt since Major died.

I'm smiling at this, pulling on my boots and about to head

out to water the garden, when Owen comes inside with a pronouncement.

"One of your chickens is gay," he deadpans.

"What!?" I squawk.

"See for yourself," he offers, opening the mudroom door and making the knowing gesture of a carnival barker at the curiosity tent.

I have heard of the fluorescent pink sheep, the world's largest pig, and the two-headed cow. But the gay chicken? This I have to see.

The Meats are lumbering around outside the garden fence, trying to get in and peck the tomatoes, but the hens are all inside their pen, right where they're supposed to be. Nine of them scratch along the edge of the coop for worms and bugs, or squat down on the ground and fluff their feathers in the dirt.

But the biggest hen of all, the one I've begun calling Alpha Chick, because she is a little bit of a bully, is standing on top of the water trough. She is arching her back and stretching out her neck as far as it will stretch. She opens her beak, almost as if she were trying to tell us something, and holds the pose for several seconds, but no sound comes out.

"Her?" I ask

"That's the one," Owen confirms.

Upon closer inspection I see that Alpha Chick has started to grow a red appendage on the top of her head that looks like a half-chewed gumball. There are a couple of emerald-green feathers sprouting from her backside that I haven't noticed before, either.

The rest of the hens are still uniform in color, a soft and lovely tan. I narrow my eye in Alpha Chick's direction, but before I can point out these physical changes to Owen, she hops off the water trough, runs straight at one of the hens taking a dirt bath—I think it's Pink Ranger—and humps her.

"Oh my God!" I yell.

"I'm telling you," Owen says, nodding.

The coupling is over quick, then Alpha Chick communicates her dominance verbally—or at least vocally. She stretches up her neck and opens up her beak again, but this time she actually speaks. And what she says is unmistakably "Cock-a-freakin'-doodle-do!"

Alpha Chick looks suspiciously like one of the roosters in Larry's poultry catalog. Alpha Chick isn't gay, I realize, because she isn't even a chick—she's a dude! As I watch her make a mad dash for Cher, I'm pretty sure that Alpha Chick is actually Alpha Chap.

"That's no lesbian!" I blurt out to Owen. "That's a rooster!"

"Whoa," he says. "For real?"

Yes, as we will all be made aware of in the coming days, for real. For very, very real.

I have learned some things in the past year about moon phases, and vegetable gardening, and, yes, even about chickens. I'm not quite so naive about all this anymore. And I know that when it comes to raising chickens for eggs or meat, roosters are nothing but an extraneous and aggressive annoyance. Hens lay just as many eggs with or without them. You need roosters if you want to hatch fertilized eggs to raise your own chicks, but other than that they're just a menace.

Over the next few days our rooster flapped his big wings and strutted, jumped the hens at will, and attacked every hand that tried to feed him. Caring for the chickens—tossing in the grain, refilling and cleaning out their water trough, raking the manure out of their pen—was a chore shared by the boys, so they were the ones taking the brunt of our rooster's testosterone flares.

And each of my sons devised his own method to outwit or outmatch him. Owen kept big rocks handy. He'd throw one at the side of the coop to create a distraction, then toss in the feed and slam the pen gate shut. If the distraction didn't work, he'd throw the rock *at* the rooster instead.

Luke was more of a chicken-wrangling stylist, and wore my tall rubber muck boots to protect his legs while waving a beach towel or a belt in figure eights like a matador, successfully fending off the bird's air attacks as well as those aimed at ankle height.

Will took his inspiration from medieval times and donned a suit of armor he cobbled together out of a cardboard box, a skateboard helmet, a wooden sword, and a trash-can lid.

"Back!" he'd order, opening the pen and striding inside, shield first. Leading with his beak or the fanglike spurs that had recently popped out of the back of his legs, the rooster never tired of attacking Will's shield. Maybe the shine infuriated him, because the *ping!* of beak on galvanized aluminum soon became a familiar sound.

"I got a name for our rooster!" Will yelled, running into the house one morning after another battle with the bird. "Pecker!" To emphasize that he had earned these naming rights, he held up his little hand, showing off the latest battle wound. Blood dripped from a V-shaped cut near his knuckle.

The double meaning of the name "Pecker" was lost on Will but not on my poor hens. With no armor, no weapons, and no chance of a diversion, they had no way to protect themselves from the gender traitor in their midst. The rooster terrorized their pebble-sized brains and their melon-sized bodies, and it was all day every day with the humping.

Pecker attacked the UPS man when he walked up the driveway to deliver the onion sets I ordered. He attacked the Meats whenever they were within range, even though they had grown to almost twice his size. He attacked leaves blowing across the yard, joggers getting in some rural miles, and two Jehovah's Witnesses whose only crime was to walk up on our porch bearing pamphlets promising, "The End of False Religion Is Near!"

As these two navy-colored suits hopped back onto their bicycles and fled, I understood another thing about roosters. If Pecker wasn't stopped soon, I could get sued for assault with a deadly chicken. Something had to be done, but what?

The next day, as I watched him run toward Gladys, I considered my options. Shoot him with the BB gun, beat him to death with that old golf club, or run him over with the minivan? Sic our big dog Super on him, put antifreeze in his water, slam the coop door on his head? Drop a cement block on him, light and toss some well-aimed firecrackers, microwave his ass?

I dismissed all of these options as the revenge fantasies of a temporarily unbalanced woman, and the boys and I gathered to brainstorm a humane end for Pecker. Execution was not off the table; we just had to devise a painless way to do it.

"Even PETA would want to kill that crazy bird," Owen says.

Despite his animal-rights stance, my oldest has been attacked one too many times, is running out of rocks, and votes in favor of Pecker's death by pretty much any means we devise.

"Yup. I vote for death, too," Will says.

His vote is contingent on two things: not having to participate in the assassination or be a witness to it.

Luke has been uncharacteristically silent during our discussion, and so I ask him what he thinks should happen to Pecker. Surprisingly, he votes for clemency, and though he doesn't exactly say why, it's probably because he's the one of the three who saw the aftermath of our pig's death.

"He doesn't think he's doing anything wrong," Luke explains. "He's just being what he is. And I don't think he should have to *die* for it."

We can respect that, and so we all agree that Luke has a week to come up with a way to spare Pecker's life, or else I will plan a humane execution. The "how" of that task is left open, and I think of the old golf club still leaning up against the barn and cringe.

So I'm relieved when the end of Pecker's reign of terror comes not with a BB-gun blast, a snap of the neck, or a tee shot, but with a whimper. Or at least the closest thing to a whimper I can imagine emanating from our rooster's abusive beak.

Luke's friend with the free-range chickens, the one who helped us move the playhouse and turn it into a coop, lives just a few miles away. In addition to chickens, his family also keeps ducks, guinea fowl, and even a peacock. If we can arrange to transport our rooster, and will throw in a bag of feed, they will adopt Pecker.

And so one weekend morning we lure the beast into Super's big wire dog kennel using green tomatoes as bait, then latch the kennel door shut and load him, lunging and squawking, into the back of the minivan. On the short drive, Pecker whirls and flops around inside the cage like a Tasmanian-devil chicken, but we arrive with him safely contained, unload the kennel, set it down on the ground, and watch as Pecker's new flock bobs on over to investigate.

Luke opens the kennel door; Pecker charges out to attack and is immediately set upon by two roosters much smaller than he is but with, we gleefully see, an obvious home advantage. Pecker fends them off, but not before losing a few feathers and taking a bloodletting beak-shot to the leg. This is exactly why it's called "pecking order," and I am satisfied to see that our rooster has been taken down a few notches. By the time we leave, Pecker is no longer trying to attack anything or anyone; he is cowering under a shrub.

Our weekend errand successfully completed, I drop the boys off at their father's before I head home to check on our hens. I thought they'd be clucking around happily in their chicken yard, doing their hen things, but instead they're scattered around the property, looking frightened and lost.

With Pecker gone, the Meats have wasted no time in pushing the hens out of the coop and taking over the nesting boxes and the fenced-in chicken yard. As usual, it looks like in trying to solve one problem, I've only succeeded in trading it in for a whole bunch of new ones.

Chicken drama will just have to wait a day. Plenty of people let their chickens range free, and tonight I just don't have time to battle the Meats. Because tonight, for once, I actually have plans.

Pete will be joining me for happy hour on the porch, where we'll discuss him finishing the remodeling project he started more than a year ago. Some of the money from the land sale will go to pay for this, but I've also been making more from my writing and editing assignments, too. The bill folder is empty, I've got a small savings account, and the well is more than half paid off.

Tonight isn't exactly a date, I don't think, because we'll be discussing business; but it isn't just an appointment, either, because I also invited him for drinks and dinner.

So what is this get-together, exactly? And why do I need to

give everything a label? Farmer vs. gardener; Christian vs. Buddhist; builder vs. boyfriend. Why can't I just *be* and let life unfold?

"To conquer oneself," the Buddha said, "is a greater task than conquering others."

I thought I *had* conquered myself, at least the part of myself that enjoys male company, when I donated my wedding dress to Goodwill. Is that the act of a woman interested in another romantic relationship? I don't think so. And yet here I am, doing something I swore I'd never, ever do again: inviting a man over.

I could have discussed the remodel with him over the phone; I didn't have to throw in dinner and drinks.

Friday happy hour on the porch is an every other-week ritual that I am used to observing all alone, often beginning one second after the boys go to Mr. W's for his "parenting time." And yet today, I have company.

There is a man leaning back in one of Grandma Link's lilac porch chairs, looking real comfortable, and watching me stride across the yard to feed the chickens. And God forgive me if I don't give him a little wiggle as I go.

What am I doing?

"Hello, girls," I say to the hens as I fling their feed in the grass. I open the door to the coop, humming, and try to shoo out the Meats, but they just run back in. I scoop chicken feed out of the metal bin and toss it on the ground; the hens cluck out their contentment, stroll back over to their pen, and peck at the yellow grain.

The Meats see the feed I'm tossing down and thunder toward me, jostling each other shoulder-to-shoulder like a pack of feathered wolves closing in. The hens flee in terror, taking cover near the barn. Something is going to have to be done about the Meats, and soon, but I already know that when the time comes, I will not be able to kill them.

I look at Pete relaxing on the porch, then back at the Meats. Pete . . . Meats. Pete . . . Meats. And I wonder.

Could he butcher chickens?

He bow-hunts for deer, he ice-fishes, he has a boat just for catching salmon out of the bay, so the answer is probably yes, and I imagine how this might go down tonight, after we're finished discussing our remodeling business and when the not-exactly-a-date part of this evening begins.

Mardi: "What do you want to do?"

Pete: "I don't know, what do *you* want to do?"

Mardi: "Oh, I don't know. Wanna butcher some chickens?"

Pete: "I thought you'd never ask!"

At which point in this fantasy he'd drop to his knees, clasp his hands together in prayer, and exclaim, "Thank you, Jesus, for delivering unto me the perfect woman."

Yeah, right.

If you count the Uncle Kracker concert and the half-dozen times Pete has anonymously plowed my driveway and the other times he's stopped by, this happy hour on my porch might qualify as a second date. Chicken butchering seems more like a sixth or seventh date, doesn't it? Or maybe even more serious than that. Maybe it's an activity reserved for a relationship that has advanced to the boyfriend/girlfriend stage.

It's no wonder I discard the idea, then. Because Lord knows, I do *not* want a boyfriend.

.   .   .

The sound of panic from somewhere outside wakes us up. Pete sits straight up like a catapult, and even half asleep I almost expect something—a boulder, a ball of flame—to be flung into the center of the bed. To be hurled our way in some form of punishment.

Not only did I invite a man over who is not my husband, and not even my boyfriend, I asked him to stay.

It's almost a full moon, and we left the windows open so a near-perfect breeze comes into my silvery bedroom. But along with this breeze comes the sounds that woke us. Frantic screeching and wings flapping.

"My hens!" is all I can yell.

But Pete is up out of my bed and halfway down the stairs in his underwear. By the time I've bolted out the front door, he is already jogging around the outside of the coop.

"I can't see anything," he yells, "but your chickens are going nuts!"

What I see are my hens, my light-brown hens, seeming to throw themselves three feet up in the air against the chicken wire. As soon as their feet touch the ground, they jump up and kamikaze again. The Meats are inside the coop, won't give up the nesting boxes, and have bullied the hens into the chicken yard.

The moon casts an eerie glow but not enough to see by, so Pete runs to his truck, starts it up, flips on his brights, and angles it so that the headlights shine directly at the coop. Framed in the fluorescent glare are fangs, two glinting eyes, and bloody feathers.

A fox has one of my hens in its mouth and is standing perfectly still. The hen's eyes are open, her beak is open too, and I can see her paralyzed little tongue. It's Mrs. Donahue, the hen I named after my kindergarten teacher.

"Hey!" Pete yells, running straight at the fox and waving his arms. The fox turns its head then, just a hair, and looks directly at Pete. It doesn't make a move to run away, it doesn't drop the hen, it just stands its ground and lifts a single front paw.

My hands reach down on the ground in the dark, and I spread my fingers out and feel for rocks. For something to throw. Sticks, tools left out, a tennis ball, anything. There is nothing, though, and the fox looks over toward the pasture, looks back toward us, and then trots away with Mrs. Donahue.

We watch its bushy tail swish back and forth like a rudder until it disappears into the waves of grass between the pasture and the woods. White feathers float in the headlight beams, my hands are on my knees, and I am panting.

It is only later that I think about Pecker. You don't need roosters for eggs; you need them to protect your hens. Pecker might have died doing it, but I know he would have taken on that fox. And Luke's words echo: *He's just being what he is.* Pecker had a purpose here, after all; he just never had the chance to fulfill it.

I think about Major, and the night he died unfolds in my mind again like a horrible slide show. Mrs. Donahue was just a chicken, not a horse I worked for and cared for and loved. But she still lived on the Big Valley and therefore was a life that I was responsible for.

You can't let your guard down for one single night, you know? I think. *Not even one.*

At least when I watch this animal about to die, I'm not doing it all alone.

.   .   .

The next morning I am expecting Pete to flee; instead, he makes us plates of steaming scrambled eggs and fried potatoes, and then gets to work fixing the holes in the chicken yard and the coop.

While he pulls boards out of the bed of his truck and finds the extra roll of chicken-wire in the barn, I fetch the mail—and pull a pretty little envelope out of the mailbox. There's the Big Valley's address in thick black ink, handwritten in my mother's perfect calligraphy.

I knew this was coming, I've been looking forward to it even, but with the land sale, and subsequent bill-paying marathon, and the Pecker extraction, and planning for the remodeling project to get going again, I've put the occasion out of my mind until now.

My parents are celebrating their fiftieth wedding anniversary with a big party. And their golden milestone just makes me feel like a failure. I am forty-five years old. Unless I meet the love of my life tomorrow and marry him the day after, I will never have a chance at a fiftieth wedding anniversary. Not ever.

And it sounds silly to admit it, but even after enduring years feeling stuck, even after my painful divorce, even after giving away my wedding dress and vowing never to get married again, I still want that. As a matter of fact, now that I know I can depend on myself, I actually want someone more than when I was afraid I wouldn't be able to handle everything alone.

I'd like a man around. Someone to share the Big Valley with, and even to share raising my sons the rest of the way with. Most startling of all, someone not just to be with, but to be married to.

I look at the invitation and know I want my own version of the kind of marriage that my parents have.

The sound of Pete's hammer on the chicken coop echoes, and

I realize there is still one hole in my life, regardless of my efforts to patch them all over.

But even if I'll never have what my parents do, I can at least get the focus off of me for one second and be happy for them. Happy that they've kept their marriage going strong for half a century. And I am happy for them, and proud of being their daughter. I'm also even a little excited about a weekend away from the Big Valley.

Priority number one over the next week is dress clothes for the boys, and as the day nears I take them shopping at, where else, Goodwill. I buy them each a pair of khaki pants and short-sleeved white button-downs. Owen and Luke still fit into the dress shoes I bought them last year to wear for their school orchestra concerts, because I bought them a half-size too big. Will is just going to have to make do with his sneakers.

To mark their special day, my Mom and Dad have invited friends and family to cruise the Saginaw Bay with them in an open-air tour boat, and then we will all head over to their church, Messiah Lutheran, for a chicken dinner.

The boys and I arrive and I watch my parents stand united on the gangplank and I love them so much it actually aches. My father's white hair is blowing in the breeze, but instead of messing it up, the wind just styles it perfectly and makes him look like he could captain this boat himself if he wanted to. Which, as a matter of fact, he could—when Ben and I were kids, our family went on weeks-long sailing vacations across Lake Huron and the Straits of Mackinac all the way to Canada. As our captain, my father was the very definition of seaworthiness, no matter the weather, the rocky moorings, the wind direction.

Standing next to him now, my mother is smiling. A genuine smile, a smile from deep inside, and it's good to see her so happy.

She is tall and regal and pretty. No, she is beautiful. Together, they greet their guests—their sailing friends, our grandpa Hain, their tall Lutheran pastor and his wife, the cousin who has gone far in advertising—and I take stock. And wonder what happened to my brother and me.

With parents like these, how could we have gone so wrong? Between Ben and me we have three marriages (one common-law), two divorces, three DUIs, five kids, two bad credit ratings, and a history of disconnected telephones. I mean, what the hell?

I ask my brother about this when I drive to the outskirts of the downstate town where he lives with his guns and his new girl-friend. I am there to pick them up—him and his girlfriend, not the guns—and give them a ride to the anniversary party, because neither of them has a valid driver's license.

"Not everyone can be like them," my brother tells me. "Not everyone wants to."

For the first time it occurs to me that he's okay with this. He's okay with the continental drift of difference between our parents' lifestyle and his own. I, on the other hand, am not. I love my farm. I love our lives there enough to go through a lot to keep them going. I can't imagine ever living anywhere else. And with the land sale, there's no doubt we've gained a little traction. But my parents have made it look easy for half a century; why does a single year of my life have to be so hard?

At the party my sons agree to help out as waiters, and they circulate among the guests with platters of cheese, crackers, and fruit. I'm proud that they're so willing to help, but quickly see that you can take the boy off the Big Valley, but you can't take the Big Valley out of the boy.

I overhear Owen bashing our country's president, George W.,

to my big grandpa Hain, whose monetary contributions to the Republican Party are legendary. In the Hain basement hangs a framed, signed color photograph of a denim-clad Ronald Reagan astride a huge chestnut gelding.

"He's not even really our president," Owen says, eating from the tray of hors d'oeuvres he is supposed to be offering to the guests. "I can't believe I might actually have to go to war someday and fight for a *fake* president."

Luke, creative as ever, has set down his tray on a deck chair and is throwing random items over the side of the tour boat: cheese slices, ice cubes, a grape, a pacifier he found on the deck. Somewhere, a baby is wailing.

"Haven't you ever seen David Letterman do 'Will It Float?' " he asks a distant cousin as I hurry by, looking for Will. I wonder how Luke has stayed up late enough to watch Mr. Letterman's program without my even knowing.

I find my youngest downstairs on the first floor of the double-decker boat, near the galley. I'm just relieved that he hasn't fallen overboard, until I watch my dad take a tip cup away from him, but not before it has been stuffed with dollar bills, presumably by my parents' guests.

Will admits that he swiped a plastic beer cup from the bar and borrowed a black marker from one of the boat's crew members to draw dollar signs all over it. He never actually *asked* anyone for money, he just rearranged the fruit, making room for the cup in the middle of his tray, then looked up at people and smiled.

"I can keep the money, right?" Will is asking my dad.

I hug my youngest as my dad looks on. My dad is not a meddler, yet now offers a rare piece of unsolicited parenting advice.

"You need to keep taking these boys to church, Mard," he says, not unkindly, then leaves to circulate.

Will stuffs the bills and change into the pocket of his used pants. A year ago, trying so hard to make us look like a normal family, I would have felt embarrassed by my sons' behavior. Not anymore. *This*, I think with some satisfaction, *is why God gave me three sons.*

Because when they are grown, Owen will know when I am too old and decrepit to farm and will take the lead in analyzing nursing-home placements; Luke will be unselfish and caring enough to come and visit me regularly there; and Will's ambition will ensure he is the one with the money to pay the bill.

Maybe I will keep taking them to church, as my father just suggested. Maybe there is a place for us inside a church and we just haven't found it yet. Or maybe they will each take up their own searches someday and find their own spiritual place. Either way, my sons have adapted like they were born to this life of grab-and-hold-on. They make no apologies for it, either, proving they've adjusted to it even better than I have.

I walk up to the top deck with Will, and he joins his brothers. They stand together, just the three of them, talking and laughing, each still doing his duty and holding his tray. I watch my triangle of boys and whatever sense of failure I've been hanging on to drifts away.

I lost my marriage, but they lost a childhood with two united parents and yet have adapted just fine. Despite the empty cupboards, the layer of ice on their bedroom windows, the carloads of firewood, the free school lunches, the sale of our land, and their parents' divorce, they are more than just fine; they are, well, wonderful. They are the very best of both of us.

I've given them everything I had in the past year, but their father probably has, too. And no milestone I pass, no victory I win, and no harvest I grow will ever be better than that. If I never in my whole life accomplish anything beyond just knowing this, it will be enough.

When we get back home, the boys and I go straight to the coop to check on the chickens. They're all fine; the anti-fox reinforcements Pete made must have worked. We feel around in the grass outside the chicken yard and find our reward: eight still-warm eggs.

After a summer of doing nothing but eating and scratching and clucking and fertilizing, our hens are finally laying eggs. And Larry was right, too, because their eggshells are an amazing blue and green. The yolks, though, are bright orange, and for the next several days I feed the boys our own scrambled eggs for breakfast. They taste the way fresh grass smells and are better than any supermarket egg ever.

With Mrs. Donahue gone, the rest of the hens stick close together, and though they wouldn't be laying eggs at all if they were overly stressed, I can still tell they would rather be inside the coop. At least at night.

The Meats aren't about to let that happen. An unsuspecting visitor would never mistake our farm for *The Big Valley* television show with them roaming free. No, they'd think they'd been dropped onto the set of a horror film starring a cast of zombified birds. The Meats seem like a completely different species, bulked up to the size of steamer trunks and bulging now as if unmentionables were hidden inside. They weigh as much as bowling balls, and their skinny legs wobble under the strain.

Not only that, but there are piles of chicken crap everywhere you step (so much for containing this by-product to use as fertilizer), and if you bend over to wipe off your shoe, expect an attack from the rear.

These, I am convinced, are the fowl descendants of the rooster whose crowing in triplicate signaled Jesus' impending betrayal. I make a farmeress decision: it's time for them to die.

I cut recipes for chicken pot pie out of the newspaper, and plan on a stuffed chicken instead of a turkey for Thanksgiving this year. I know exactly which chicken I want to invite to our table for the holiday: the one with a thing for ankles.

"I'll fix your little red wagon, pal," I promise.

My brother gave us his freezer, it runs fine, and I have big plans to pack it full of legs, thighs, breasts, and roasters. I consider calling Pete to do the deed, decide we are not yet to this place in our new relationship, and sit down with the Yellow Pages instead and look up "butchers."

It takes a few phone calls, but someone finally explains that I'm not going to be able to find a commercial butcher to come to my farm and slaughter my chickens. Michigan's legislature has outlawed farm calls. Which means meat retailers are no longer allowed to come to your farm and kill stuff. Now, you either have to kill your livestock yourself or take it to a USDA-inspected meat-processing plant. The closest one to me is outside Grand Rapids, 160 miles south.

The prospect of three hours of highway driving accompanied by fifteen angry bowling balls with feathers, beaks, and leg spurs is not a trip I relish or even contemplate. I've got to talk to Larry.

"Land sakes, girl!" he bellows from the help desk, tiring by now, I'm sure, of my relentless questions. "You can kill a chicken!

Get a funnel, stick the heads in, chop 'em off, let 'em drain, parboil the feathers off, gut 'em, bag 'em, and toss 'em in the freezer for the winter!"

I have been reliving this gruesome scenario ever since I was twelve years old and unwittingly scarfed down Thumper's deep-fried hindquarters at my grandma Link's kitchen table. What made me think that I am any different at forty-five than I was at twelve?

I couldn't kill a hog last fall, and I don't think I can unleash the big "S" today on a chicken, either. Maybe I would be able to kill one if it had on a black balaclava and was coming at me in my bedroom in the dark with a knife, but I know myself, and I know I cannot kill fifteen chickens. Not without years of therapy anyway and I don't have that kind of time.

As brutal as my fowl charges have turned out to be, I still raised the Meats from tiny babies. I can eat them, but I can't murder them, hypocritical as that may be. Instead, I stop at the cashier on the way out of Tractor Supply and pay for another forty-pound bag of chicken feed.

The meat portion of our chicken-raising experiment has obviously gone off the rails. Just when they were beginning to relax with Pecker gone, my sons are being attacked in their own yard again, our entire wardrobe of footwear is ruined, and, at eleven dollars a bag for feed, the costs are mounting. Maybe, I think, there is someone noncommercial, who would consider doing the deed.

I call the 4-H, the local food co-op, an organic rabbit farm, and a commune in the next county. Will anyone butcher my chickens? "Too late," "Don't do it," "Too messy," and "Dude, we're vegans" are my answers.

I let the Meats roam during the day and they stray to a distant neighbor's yard and scratch up her landscape mulch. She no longer waves when she sees me at my mailbox. Their drumsticks, I am convinced, are getting tougher by the day, and they have pecked all the grapes off my grapevine. They drink the water out of my landscape pond and terrify the koi. Even the stray cats fear them.

On a day I shoo the Meats out of the road where they have stopped traffic, my brother has apparently gotten his driver's license back, because he arrives for an impromptu visit.

"Those are pit-bull chickens!" he says, hurrying into my house and slamming the door.

I hug him. "Please kill them," I say, thinking of his gun collection.

Finally, a solution. Why didn't I think of it earlier? Ben is the consummate fisherman and hunter. If you go to his trailer for dinner, you will be served fish or game. Might be bluegill, might be lake trout, might be venison, might even be rabbit, but it will be tasty and it will be something he shot or hooked or trapped or snared. Once I opened his refrigerator door on a whim and found a six-pack of Schlitz and a foil-wrapped mass shaped exactly like a squirrel, tail included. "Bacon-wrapped," he said, "they ain't half bad."

Ben is not a workingman whose hobby is hunting; he is a hunting man whose hobby is working. Butchering chickens should be like flicking June bugs into a bucket for him.

"No problem," he says.

My brother *can* do the big "S." At last! A chicken hit man has not only been identified, but contracted, too. What a relief!

But three days later, despite frequent reminders from me, the Meats are still roaming the countryside like a gang of Nazi youth.

And while I'm out running errands, my brother packs up and leaves for bigger game. He's meeting some buddies farther north to scout deer blind sites for fall. All the beer in my refrigerator is gone. That is the way of the hunter.

I have now been betrayed by my government, local merchants, the 4-H, the hippies, and even my own family. For this, I am not above asking for help.

God, I pray before I go to sleep that night, *please smite the Meats. Smite them hard and smite them now.*

The next morning when I open my front door, they are on the threshold. I call the newspaper and pay for a one-day advertisement to run on Saturday in the classifieds. It contains my phone number and simply reads:

FREE.

LIVE MEAT CHICKENS.

YOU PICK UP.

On Saturday morning at 6:30 the phone rings.

"You still have chickens?" a man asks.

"Yes, I still have chickens," I answer. "Please, in the name of all that's holy, come and get them."

"I will," he replies.

The day scratches on without chicken removal. But after dark, just as I have given up hope, a small pickup truck pulls into the driveway. Our dog Friday barks as if signaling the apocalypse and there is a knock on the door. I open it and see a muscular and handsome middle-aged man in jeans and a trucker hat. He has black hair and black eyes.

"I am here," he says. He is my savior.

I grab a flashlight. The door to the pickup truck opens and two young men, an old woman, and a little girl get out. The apostles, I think. We walk to the coop, where the Meats are sleeping. My poor hens are huddling together as usual, just outside.

The two younger men are dressed as if they were about to appear in a music video: oversized leather jackets and baggy jeans, chain wallets, baseball caps turned to the side. They cross their rangy arms over their chests. They *so* do not want to be here, boxing up free chickens. One look from the savior, though, and that is what they do.

The old woman is expressionless, but she nods to me and I nod back. I smile at the little girl and she turns her face into the hood of her jacket. They speak to each other in Spanish. The man, my savior, is the only one who speaks to me.

"My family eats well tomorrow," he says, and shakes my hand.

All spring and all summer I was raising meat for them and I didn't even know it. I thought I was doing something for myself and for my family. I wasn't. I was doing it for him and for his family.

It has taken us a whole year, twelve full moons have come and gone, but our circumstances have shifted, just a little. My moon is waxing now, not waning anymore.

A year ago I would have served the wild turkey that Owen hit with our car, and now I'm giving away good meat to a family that might need it even more than we do.

This, I think, *this present moment, this is what a good harvest feels like.*

It wasn't only a farm that needed saving a year ago; it was a family. It was all four of us.

My savior, the apostles, and the Meats all get back in the

pickup truck and drive away. I watch until their taillights disappear at the end of my driveway. I shine the flashlight into the coop. The hens have already moved back in, and snuggle together in the nesting boxes. I think back to when they were just baby chicks, just yellow cotton balls with eyes.

Maybe God thinks of me and my sons this way.

"Safe and sound," I say. "We are all safe and sound."

Epilogue

August 2010

BLUE MOON

Blue Moon: An extra full moon that occurs in a season.
Also colloquially means a rare event, reflected in the phrase
"once in a blue moon."

—Farmers' Almanac

Through my bedroom window I hear the lazy afternoon hum of cicadas in the old elm tree, mixing together with a goldfinch's cheery song and the excited whispering of the last guests to arrive.

There's a pause, time slows, then I hear Owen launch into "Over the Rainbow" on his cello and my heart vibrates. That's my cue.

I walk down the stairs and there's Luke and Will, waiting for me at the bottom and grinning. They're handsome in their new khakis, white collared shirts tucked in, and leather belts. Their thick hair, often so unruly, is combed and smooth. They smell like soap. Luke has polished his new dress shoes, but Will is wearing flip-flops.

"I can't find my other shoes," he whispers, as if he is already anticipating my irritation, but I hardly notice.

Even with heels on I have to stand on my tiptoes to kiss the top of Will's blond head. But flip-flops are fine, field flowers are fine, dancing in a barn is just fine, too. Pete is waiting, so it's all just fine by me.

My sons hook their arms in mine and we walk out our front door and onto our porch and down the length of it until we stop in the middle. My porch posts are decorated with beautiful paper flowers handmade by my mother, and the railing is draped with yards and yards of orange and white gingham. Our guests stand in the front lawn, smiling at our second chance, and the late-summer sun shines on their faces.

A local poet, ordained via the magic of the Internet, looks smart in his paisley vest and bow tie. He faces the crowd, the Good Book open, and begins to read from the Song of Solomon.

"Arise, my darling, my beautiful one, and come along. For behold, the winter is past, the rain is over and gone. The flowers have already appeared and the voice of the turtledove has been heard in our land.

"Arise, my darling, my beautiful one, And come along!"

The door at the other end of the porch opens and out walks Pete in a black suit, his two grown sons in khaki and white too, and they join Luke, Will, and me on our porch. Owen stops playing, puts down his cello bow, and joins us. Together we are a bride, a groom, and our five solid sons. Together, we are a family.

"Welcome!" the Poet says.

Pete takes both my hands in his and looks into my face. Walt Whitman and Emily Dickinson are our witnesses, then more pretty things are said that I don't remember clearly, because I am too happy.

"Repeat after me . . ." the Poet says. Pete turns to face the assembled crowd, grins at my parents and then at our family and friends.

"I, Pete!" he bellows, with a surety that fills up my whole body. Shoulders back, chin up, his hands relax over the porch railing as he says, "Take you, Mardi."

He takes me, I think. He's seen a fox run off with one of my chickens, he's heard me on the phone negotiating with bill collectors, he likes his own farmhouse but knows what the Big Valley means to me and agrees we'll live here.

He knows me and yet still he takes me. *Me.*

Nearly five years ago he and I shared one of the worst days of our lives and now we're sharing one of the best.

Then this man I love and am in love with slides a pear-shaped diamond ring on my finger. The Poet can hardly get the words out before I take Pete, I *so* take him for me, and then we are married, and then we are kissing.

"I'd like to present to you—HOOONNNNKKK!"

The Poet is about to say, "I'd like to present to you Pete and Mardi, husband and wife," when the ceremony is interrupted.

A huge semi truck drives by and blows its horn. Loud.

My road is on a hill and this truck is on the downslope, and the driver must have seen all the flowers and my white cotton dress and the big crowd gathered, because he blows that sucker for a really, *really* long time. It echoes down the hill and into the valley long after he has passed by.

"I'd like to present to you—HOOONNNNKKK!"

All of our guests are giggling or at least grinning. All five of our sons are laughing so hard that not one of them is standing up straight. My father has his arm around my mother and her mouth is open in an O, but she is smiling too, as big as anyone.

"Is it always going to be like this when I kiss you?" I ask my new husband.

I ask him this softly, while people are laughing, and I speak it close to his ear so no one else can hear me.

"Most women would be happy with fireworks," he whispers back. "Or rice, or a honeymoon."

"I'm not most women."

"Don't I know it."

I look into his whole face and remind myself, *Be aware of your surroundings*. And I will this moment to last. I will it into a present that I can open again and again whenever I want to. Inside will be the laughter of our sons and the safety of our little farm and a love so surprising it feels just like the blast of a horn.

Author's Note

This is a work of nonfiction. The events depicted really happened and really happened to my sons and me. I wish some of them hadn't, but to quote my wise grandpa Hain, "Sometimes you just get what you get."

All dialogue is from memory, and I've been told that I have a pretty good one for that kind of thing—a level of recall that has inspired observations such as "Man, you never forget *anything*, do you?"

Some names have been changed, and there is one composite character: Pecker the rooster. Dates, facts, and dollar amounts are from district court records, tax returns, public-school attendance records, a police report, insurance papers, a divorce decree, canceled checks, shutoff notices, concert tickets, land deeds, well-drilling invoices, a mortgage application, and wedding photos.

Acknowledgments

If you are a single mother in the heartland, trying to make a go of your questionable choices while writing about them, here is what I would suggest:

First, raise a trio of undaunted sons like Owen, Luke, and Will. Raise sons unafraid of dirt, cold, their mother's tears, public opinion, or hard work. Raise sons who celebrate with you, when you have secured a book deal, by cheering, as Will did, in this way: "Yeah! No more government cheese!"

Raise sons who love you despite your ridiculous self, who support your writing by turning down their guitar amplifiers during your working hours. Raise sons who you just know will be the very best kind of men when they are grown—smart, compassionate, funny, and resourceful. (I'd tell you how good-looking they are, too, except that I still have to live with them.)

But even before that, have Marylyn and Chuck Link as your parents, and Florence Link and Richard Hain as your grandparents. These capable people will not tolerate your smart mouth or you rolling your sarcastic teenage eyes, but will take you to dude ranches and on wilderness horseback trips, send you to journalism school (and pay for it), buy you warm coats, pass on their cookbook and their reverence for the land, for Michigan, and will even try to teach you the value of a dollar, which, to your peril, you will take a very long time to learn.

Next, try to carry a marriage for twenty years and fail. Swear off men forever, don't date, and recoil in horror when your friends suggest you create something called an online dating profile. Lust after Pete instead, the cabinetmaker you hire to build an addition onto your century-old farmhouse. Fall for him hard as timber. Marry him. Proceed to love him to pieces.

Get help and good advice from writers whose talent is surpassed only by their generosity. These would include Anya Achtenberg, Fleda Brown, Elizabeth Buzzelli, Lynn Hugo, Phillip Lopate, Thomas Lynch, Richard McCann, Emily Meier, Aimé Merizon, Cari Noga, Anne-Marie Oomen, Teresa Scollon, Heather Shumaker, Aaron Stander, Doug Stanton, Keith Taylor, Carolyn Walker, and, most especially, smudge sister Mary Ellen Geist.

Raise your writer's hand as high as you can so that you can be noticed way out here in the Midwest by the determined, smart, and miraculous Jane Dystel and everyone at DGLM. Have her show your words to editor Jordan Pavlin, a woman who hears them and understands them and teaches you that that's the very best you can hope for as a writer: to be heard and understood; to be able to say, "This is how it was—and we survived it."

Mardi Jo Link is the author of *When Evil Came to Good Hart* (2008) and *Isadore's Secret* (2009), winner of the Michigan Notable Book Award. She lives with her sons and husband on the Big Valley, a farm in northern Michigan.

A NOTE ON THE TYPE

This book was set in Adobe Garamond. Designed for the Adobe Corporation by Robert Slimbach, the fonts are based on types first cut by Claude Garamond (c. 1480–1561).

Typeset by Scribe,
Philadelphia, Pennsylvania
Printed and bound by Berryville Graphics,
Berryville, Virginia
Designed by Soonyoung Kwon